PRINT YOUR OWN FABRIC

By Linda Turner Griepentrog and Missy Shepler

Kaleidoscope Kutz image

©2007 by Linda Turner Griepentrog and Missy Shepler
Published by

kp krause publications
An Imprint of F+W Publications

700 East State Street • Iola, WI 54990-0001
715-445-2214 • 888-457-2873
www.krausebooks.com

Our toll-free number to place an order or obtain a free catalog is (800) 258-0929.

The following trademarked terms and companies appear in this publication:
Adobe®, ArcSoft®, Artchix Studio, Artistrywear™, Aurifil, Blumenthal Lansing™, Bubble Jet Set 2000™, Bubble Jet Set™ Rinse, C. Jenkins Necktie & Chemical Co., Canon® Print Planet, Clipart.com™, Clotilde's Sewing Savvy™, Clover USA, Color Textiles®, Computer Printer Fabric™, Corel®, Craft Fuse®, Crafter's Pick™ The Ultimate! Glue, Creek Bank Creations, Design Originals, Dick Blick, Dharma Trading Co., Dover Publications, Electric Quilt Co., Epson, ExtravOrganza™, Fabric Traditions™, Fredrix®, HeatnBond™, HeatnBond™Lite, Hewlett-Packard®, Home Arts, Husqvarna Viking, Inkssentials™, Jacquard® Products, June Tailor®, Kaleidoscope Collections, Kaleidoscope Kreator™, Kandi® Corp., KK2000™, Krause™ Publications, Krylon®, Macintosh, Mallery Press™, McGonigal Paper, Memory Frames™, Microsoft®, Miss Mary's Quaint & Curious Clip Art, National Geographic™, Nikon™ Coolpix, onOne™, Orvus™, Pellon®, Peltex, Pentel®, PhotoShapes, Photoshop®, Photoshop® Elements, Picasa™, Pix Pen™, Plaid® Enterprises, Poly-Fil™, Poster Software, PrintOnIt.com, Printed Treasures™, PROchemical, Prym™ Consumer USA, Quick Art®, Quick Fuse™, Quilter's Art, Quiltgard™, QuiltSmart®, Ranger Industries, Robert Kaufman Fabrics, Schiffer™ Publishing, Scotchgard™, Scraplight™, ScrapSmart®, Search Press, Sew News™, Sew Paintable™, Sewing Basket Fun, Snickerdoodle Dreams, Soft Expressions, Soft Fabric Photos, Steam-A-Seam2®, Sudberry House, Sulky®, Synthrapol™, The Vintage Workshop™, The Warm™ Company, Therm O Web, Traditions Studio, Two Peas in a Bucket, Veer™, Warm & Natural™, Warm & White™, Weeks Dye Works, Windows®, Wisconsin Lighting, Yahoo®, You've Been Framed™, Z Becky Brown™

Library of Congress Catalog Number: 2006934236

ISBN-13: 978-0-89689-247-7
ISBN-10: 0-89689-247-6

Designed by Rachael Knier
Edited by Erica Swanson

Printed in China

Acknowledgments

This book has come together with the help of many people who deserve thanks. First, to Jeanine Twigg, who suggested that I write it when I didn't have the confidence to write about a "technology" subject — my name associated with technology is a true oxymoron. But if you think about it, who better to communicate with the non-techies of the world than another non-techie?

Many thanks go to my friend and co-author Missy Shepler for always being there to answer computer-related questions, no matter how dumb they sounded. She has the ability to help without being condescending, though I suspect that sometimes she may be secretly laughing to herself at the things I ask.

Without art, this book would not exist. Kudos to contributing artists Alison Winn, Missy and Scott Shepler (not only does Missy know about computers, but she's a talented artist as well), Micky Turner, Mellisa Karlin Mahoney, and the talented folks at The Vintage Workshop and ScrapSmart. Read more about them on page 132.

In addition, thanks to family and friends who gave us their treasured photographs to use.

Thanks go to the many industry companies who contributed products for photography and projects as well; check out their names in the directory on page 136.

I credit my sister Micky Turner with the inspiration for this book. Without her colorful kaleidoscope imagery and creative photography, this book never would have happened. She also taught me to use basic graphics software so I could do fun things with images.

Continuing thanks go to my wonderful husband Keith, who encouraged me to take on this project, supported my experimental efforts to step outside the box and sometimes laughed when I said "I wonder what would happen if I … ?". I'm sure he was often dubious of my using the office equipment in non-traditional ways, but he always urged me to try something new — as long as I didn't damage anything!

Thanks to my mom as well. Though she doesn't understand that writing can be a living and only knows enough about computers to look at the imagery on the screen, she instilled in me a great sense of adventure to try new things and challenge myself intellectually.

— Linda

Acknowledgments

Wow!

That's what I said when Linda asked me to partner on this book. I was deeply honored by her request, but I was a little doubtful that I could pull it off. After all, even though I loved quilting and creating stitched projects, I was a newbie compared to Linda.

But I bit, and when Linda showed me some of her projects, I said "Wow" again. Her printed pieces were bold, bright, colorful creations that screamed sheer fun. I couldn't wait to try this cool technique myself.

It wasn't long before I fell prey to the "What if … ?" wonder. I began hoarding my printer ink and making even more excuses to visit local fabric shops. (It's research, honey. Really.) At last, here was a project where my inner geek could complement my artsy side.

I will always be indebted to Linda and amazed that she gave me this incredible opportunity — I can't thank her enough for including me in the fun. Thanks also to everyone at Krause Publications for patiently guiding me through the publishing task and putting up with my design suggestions. Extra-special thanks go to my family and friends, who waited for me to reappear from whatever creative abyss I'd been lost in while I was printing, stitching and wondering "What if … ?". It means the world that they are still here now that I'm out.

— *Missy*

CD-ROM image coneflower.jpg

Table of Contents

Introduction

Who would have thought that I'd be writing a book about anything to do with computers? When I was hired as the editor of Sew News magazine in 1985, my desk came equipped with an IBM electric typewriter with an auto-correct feature to back itself up and fix mistakes invisibly. To me, that was high-tech! Anyone who knows me would agree — I don't jump on the new technology bandwagon.

How did I, the techno-phobe, get into designing fabric using an inkjet printer? Actually, as much as I love fabrics of all kinds, I used to have little interest in making my own.

I first saw the possibilities of fabric printing when I moved to Oregon in 2003 and found that my sister, an avid photographer, had figured out a way to shoot imagery through a teleidoscope (a close relative to the kaleidoscope). She screws a special lens to her camera to create fabulously intricate and fractionated imagery, sure to intrigue and inspire. For example, a bowl of ordinary strawberries becomes a work of art; a simple flower blossom, a medium of intrigue; and a pieced quilt pattern, a project even more complex than the artist intended. Sometimes the new images don't look anything like the original subject!

So, I'm blaming my fabric printing compulsion on my sister Micky! She's not a sewer, so she didn't think about transferring her beautiful imagery to fabric. I convinced her that there was tremendous potential among fabric artists to create wonderful projects using her images, and my persuasion led to her current business, Kaleidoscope Kutz. It sells design CD-ROMs to quilters and other artisans, who use them for printing on all kinds of fabric, paper and other media, including metal — all done using inkjet printers.

Can you guess what these are? They are a crocus, a fern and silk flowers shot through a teleidoscope.

At the same time, other companies in the sewing industry were creating all sorts of image collections, from elegant monograms to licensed whimsical motifs.

Since I wanted to manipulate images and create fabric, I had to learn something about computer technology. Enter self-doubt and stomach knots! I was already savvy about getting words onto a page, but I didn't know how to get images where I wanted them to be on fabric — only visions for the finished product.

Sewers — at least the ones I know — tend to learn things for a specific purpose. You don't need extensive computer skills to print on fabric. In fact, you can print on fabric without a computer at all if you have an all-in-one machine or an inkjet copier. All you need is desire, and you'll figure out how to accomplish the task. My friend and former Hewlett-Packard education manager, Joe Hesch, helped me overcome my fear and master some fun printing tasks. We continue to inspire each other!

My sewing industry experience has shown me that sewers are strongly motivated to try new things. Learning to print on fabric is no harder than mastering the skill of making do with less fabric than the pattern requires. Don't be afraid to try!

This book is not brand-specific, nor does it give instruction for specific software programs. Instead, we've focused on the capabilities of current printing and software programs in our changing technological world. We've also added fun techniques to inspire you to forget any fears and just get started.

Have fun experimenting with the original art on the enclosed CD-ROM as well as the commercial images featured throughout the book. Then go forth with your new knowledge and play!

— *Linda*

Look for Missy and Linda resting in our respective chairs, now that this book is done!

Kathy Schmitz, Quilter's Art image; colored with fabric markers

CHAPTER 1
GETTING STARTED

You can use this basic equipment for printing images or text on fabric.

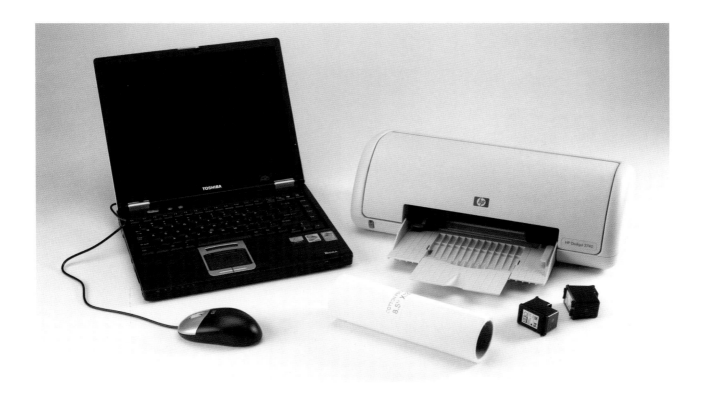

Being able to print your own fabric is the ultimate creative high for any sewer. There are many wonderful fabrics available and tons of techniques for traditional methods of patterning and printing fabrics, but being able to conceptualize something and make it happen on the fabric is great fun.

You can print anything on fabric that you can print on paper — soda straws; a fragile, not-so-well preserved photograph of your ancestors; a colorful mix of sewing tools; or even your hand pressed against the scanner or copier bed (remember those college pranks?).

Why print directly on the fabric instead of using an iron-on transfer? Transfers can change the hand of the fabric, often making it feel more rigid, shiny and inflexible. Printing directly on the fabric does not change the feel or drape of the fabric.

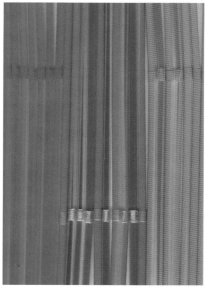

Colorful straws create fun texture.

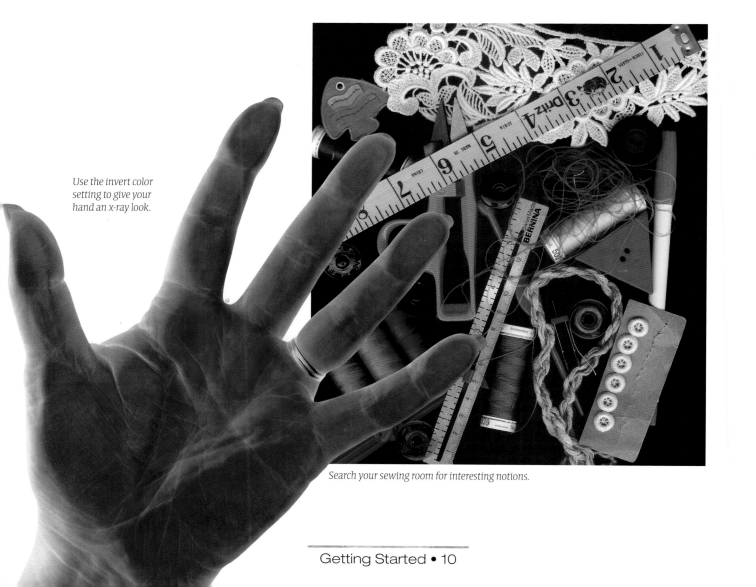

Use the invert color setting to give your hand an x-ray look.

Search your sewing room for interesting notions.

Inkjet Printers

An inkjet printer is crucial for printing your own fabric. It's important to note that this book deals only with inkjet technology, not laser or dye sublimation technology.

Letter size (8 ½" x 11") is the most commonly used print size in the U.S. A4 (8 ¼" x 11 ¾") is a common European size. All of the projects in this book can be created with either A4 or letter-sized prints, or extended file lengths only.

The surge in consumer digital camera use has made smaller format printers popular. Photo printers capable of printing borderless 4" x 6" images can provide a quick, convenient and portable solution for creating single quilt blocks, postcards, greeting card images and other small items.

Most fabric artists aspire to have wide-format printers in their sewing rooms because making larger projects from 8 ½" x 11" sheets requires tedious piecing. Once you're hooked on fabric printing, you'll want a printer that can print at least 11" x 17" or 13" x 19" files to reduce the seaming needed for large quilts and garments. The popularity of scrapbooking has made 12"-wide printers commonplace.

There are many brands of inkjet printers available. Print quality and options vary according to manufacturer and model. Some companies do not recommend using their products for fabric printing. Read the instructions and warranty information included with your printer to learn which restrictions may apply. You may need to visit the manufacturer's Web site or call the company to confirm that printing on fabric will not void the printer warranty.

Inkjet, Laser and Dye Sub

The main difference between these three digital printing processes is how the ink or dye is transferred to the paper. Inkjet printers spray millions of tiny ink droplets onto the surface of the paper (or fabric). Laser printers use tiny lasers and static electricity to transfer powdered toner (electrically-charged pigment and plastic) to paper, and then they fuse the toner onto the page with heated rollers. Photocopiers work much the same way. Dye sublimation printers (often called "dye sub printers") use a heating head to vaporize (or sublimate) solid color dye, creating a tiny gaseous cloud that is absorbed into the paper or fabric.

Thinking of buying a new printer? See "Planning to Purchase" in the Tech Tips for helpful hints.

Multi-Function Machines

These home-office workhorses, often called all-in-ones, include copying, scanning, printing and/or faxing functions, and can operate with or without a computer.

As scanners, they capture images of anything placed on the scanner bed. If the scanner is connected to a computer, you can save the scanned image file for later manipulation.

As copiers, they print an image of anything placed on the bed directly to the fabric.

As printers, they transfer images sent from the computer to the fabric.

Some all-in-ones allow you to change image size to common pre-set photo sizes (4" x 6" or 5" x 7", etc.), enlarge or reduce image size by percentages, group multiple images per page, lighten or darken images, and adjust image sharpness and print quality. Some can print proof sheets, tile poster-sized prints, banner images, reverse or mirror images, and more. Most machines also offer the option of printing on several types of media, including heavier papers (which translates to fabric for sewers!) and iron-on transfer sheets (where the image is reversed automatically so that it will appear correctly on the fabric). Available features vary between brands and models.

Some all-in-ones feature card slots, which allow the machine to print directly from a digital camera's memory card. Not all machines accept all cards. Check for camera card compatibility before you buy.

Copiers

Inkjet copiers are another option for imprinting an image to fabric. If your copier has a flat bed, anything placed on the bed of the copier will be printed on the fabric — from photos to packing peanuts.

Have It Printed for You

If you want fabric printed but would prefer not to do it yourself, many quilt shops, copy centers, and scrapbooking, fabric and craft stores will print it for you. Some shops will also help you alter images before printing — restoring old photos to better condition, sharpening image quality, changing image lightness or darkness, enhancing colors, reducing red-eye, etc.

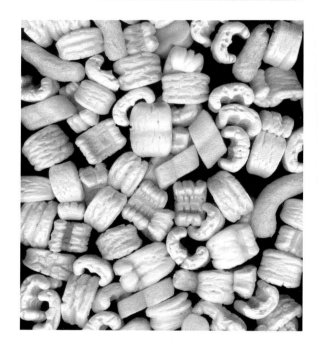

Elizabeth Barry photo

About Ink

Most inkjet printers use either pigment- or dye-based inks, or a combination of both (one kind for the color ink and another for the black ink).

Both types of ink have two main components — a colorant and a carrier. The colorant, as its name suggests, gives the ink its color. The carrier is simply a transport medium. It contains the colorant, along with a few other ingredients designed to help the colorant penetrate and stick to the paper or fabric surface.

Dye-based inks have colorants made of tiny molecules which penetrate paper or fabric fibers to create rich, smooth, uniform images. Pigment inks contain larger colorants that sit on top of the paper or fabric surface, forming a film or layer where the ink is applied.

Which is better? Each type of ink has its own strengths and weaknesses. Dyes tend to have a greater color range, print rich uniform images and stand up well to repeated washings, but they may be more susceptible to light fading, humidity and pollution. Pigments tend to be more lightfast and less sensitive to humidity and other environmental factors, but they can look slightly weaker or duller than dye-based inks. Pigment inks can abrade or rub off, making them a poor choice for wearables or other items that may be washed frequently. Pigment inks can also "settle out" or separate over time, causing inconsistent color prints.

In an effort to improve their products, printer manufacturers change ink formulas from time to time; so as a result, the differences between pigment- and dye-based inks are diminishing.

CD-ROM image cosmetic.jpg

Dye or Pigment?

How do you know what type of ink your printer uses?

If you were able to view your printouts under a very powerful microscope, you would be able to see a difference between dye- and pigment-based inks. The dye-based inks would appear as a smooth surface, while the pigment-based inks would create a raised surface where applied to the paper or fabric.

Most manufacturers don't indicate the type of ink used in their printers. You may need to contact the manufacturer to find out what type of ink is used in your printer model.

Print Permanence

With the increased popularity of digital printing, many people are concerned about print permanence. How long will the image last? Will the images fade?

The simple answer is ... we don't know! Compared to traditional textile printing, digital inkjet printing is a fairly new medium. Although testing is underway, most experiments focus on manufacturer-specific inks and papers that were designed to work together to create a lasting print. Substituting fabric (either ready-to-print or self-prepared) for the tested paper alters print results.

Until testing is done on inkjet *fabric* printing, we can't say for sure how long a print will last. We do know that environmental factors, such as light, heat, humidity and even air pollution can cause inkjet prints to fade. To keep your printed fabric projects looking their best, follow these simple rules:

Sunlight exposure and repeated washing can fade inkjet prints.

- Comply with manufacturer's directions for printing and post treatment to get the best possible results.

- Print only on fabric that has been chemically treated to accept the inks. You can print on non-treated fabrics, but the inks will not be permanent.

- Keep prints out of direct sunlight. Store projects away from light in a drawer or acid-free box.

- When washing printed pieces, use a mild detergent, such as Orvus soap, Synthrapol or Bubble Jet Rinse. If washing by machine, use cold water on a delicate cycle. Limit agitation time, and steer clear of detergents with optical brighteners. Do not dry-clean unless the fabric manufacturer specifically recommends the process.

- If possible, allow your printed projects to air dry on an absorbent towel. If you must use a dryer, throw an old towel in as well to help prevent the printed fabric from folding back on itself and transferring ink to another surface.

- Use a protective coating or spray, such as Quiltgard or Scotchgard Fabric Protector, if your finished item will be subjected to a lot of handling.

Gathering Images

If you'd like to incorporate your own images into a printed project, add a scanner or digital camera to your tool arsenal. These devices make it easy to capture and create images from everyday items in the world around you. Add an image-editing program, and you've got the ingredients for a creative fabric studio!

Scanners

As previously mentioned, some all-in-one machines include scanning capabilities. Other scanners are peripheral devices that must be connected to a computer. Like printers, there are many brands and models available, ranging from small hand-held devices to high-end professional machines for the publishing industry.

Most desktop scanners are flatbed scanners, consisting of a box topped with a glass plate to cover the scanner elements. Your image or object is placed on the glass, and scanner sensors move down the length of the bed, scanning and transforming what they "see" into digital information the computer can understand. Some flatbed scanners can scan transparent media, such as film negatives, slides and transparencies.

Sheet-fed scanners accept only flat media, which limits what can be scanned with those devices.

Most scanning software allows you to choose the color space, resolution and scale of your scan. Basic color spaces include standard RGB (Red, Green, Blue), Grayscale and Line Art (or 1-color). RGB is used for color scans with millions or billions of colors, Grayscale interprets the image or object on the scanner bed as shades of gray, and Line Art assigns one color, either black or white, to each scanned pixel. Your scanner may even have additional color space options.

Send out for Scans

Not everyone has a scanner — and not everyone wants to scan his or her own images. A number of scanning services, from professional digitizers to one-hour photo labs, are available.

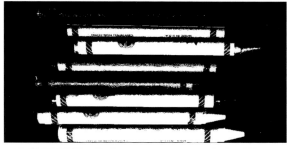

Resolution determines the amount of information the scanner captures, so it directly impacts the quality of your scan. Higher resolution means more detail ... and a larger file size.

Scaling refers to the physical size of a scan. If you set the scale at 100%, objects will be scanned at their actual size. At 50%, objects will be half their actual size, and at 200%, objects will be twice their actual size.

In general, it's a good idea to "scan high" to capture the most detail and information in your images, especially if you're not sure exactly how the final image will be used. The goal in creating image files is to make a file that has enough information to make a pleasing image, but not any more data than you need. Larger file sizes eat up hard drive space, take longer to manipulate in image-editing software, and may be harder and slower to print.

Experiment! Scan the same image or object using a variety of settings, and compare your results. Keep notes of the various settings, and save your results for future reference.

Scan objects at different sizes and compare results in an image editing program.

Learn more about how scanners capture and convert images in Tech Tip 2.

Digital Cameras

Once the exclusive tools of professional photographers, digital cameras have become less expensive and more widely available in recent years. Like film cameras, digital cameras use a lens, shutter and focusing mechanism; but instead of housing light-reactive film to capture an image, digital cameras contain electronic components necessary for capturing, processing and storing image information. Exact components vary, depending on the quality and type of camera. In general, a digital camera works much like a miniature scanner, using light reflected from an object onto a sensor. Image information is converted to a digital format and saved on the camera in an attached storage media, such as a memory card or miniature hard drive, or downloaded to a host computer.

Image quality is related to the number of pixels — or resolution — that a camera can record. Higher resolution usually means better image quality — and a correspondingly high price. Manufacturers often indicate digital camera resolution in terms of megapixels, or millions of pixels. Megapixel resolution is determined by multiplying the number of pixels in the capture area (width and height), and then dividing by one million.

Megapixel	Pixel area (width x height)	Optimum print size
0.3 Megapixels	640 x 480	Screen quality only
1.2 Megapixels	1280 x 960	4" x 6", 5" x 7"
2.1 Megapixels	1600 x 1200	5" x 7"
3.3 Megapixels	2048 x 1536	8" x 10"

Chart information from Epson.com

CHAPTER 2
IMAGINE THE POSSIBILITIES

We're bombarded with imagery every day; we observe the images in our world from the moment we open our eyes in the morning until we go to sleep at night. Even then, we may "see" images in our dreams.

Imagery Basics

Most digital images are bitmap images composed of pixels (*pic*ture *el*ements) arranged on a grid. Each pixel is assigned a specific location and color value. The more pixels in an image, the more detailed the image appears. The number of pixels determines an image's resolution. If there are 72 pixels across one inch of an image, the image has a resolution of 72ppi, or 72 pixels per inch. The higher the number of pixels per inch, the more detailed the image appears.

The physical size, resolution and intended use of an image determine how large an image can be printed before it starts to pixelate or degrade. For fabric printing, images should have a resolution of at least 150ppi — preferably 200 or 300ppi — for printing at actual size. If you plan to enlarge the image for a poster or banner, it should have even greater resolution.

The image you print on fabric can come from any number of places. Whatever the source, be sure you have the right to print it. Even though an image exists and you have the technology to reproduce it, you don't have the legal right to copy it.

Bought and Sold

You don't have to be an artist to print your own fabric. Many companies offer resources that make it easy to create fabulous one-of-a-kind fabric prints. You can purchase photographs and clip art image collections on CD-ROMs. Individual images can be downloaded from Web sites. Permission-free clip art books contain reproducible images, and some specialty software offers ready-to-print items.

Enlarge an image in your editing program to view individual pixels.

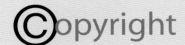opyright

The Circled C

Copyrights protect the originator of artwork from unauthorized use. In general, the copyright law protects original work for 70 years after the author's death. After that, the work becomes public domain unless the copyright is renewed.

Many artists will grant you permission to use copies of their work for personal purposes, such as adding a pocket to a child's garment with their favorite character on it, but will not permit you to present the imagery as your own or package it for resale in any form. Some license agreements, like those for Disney characters, do not allow personal use at all, and these prohibitions are strictly enforced.

Some artwork is licensed only for a single use. For example, machine embroidery motifs may be licensed only for embroidery usage. Scanning or printing the embroidery motif may be a violation of copyright law.

Purchasing a printed item does not give you the right to reproduce it. Tempting as it may be to scan your vacation postcards to make an album cover, it is not technically legal to do so. Those photographs belong to someone else. Instead, look for copyright-free images of your vacation destination, or use photographs you took on your visit. Even cute school kid pics and candid wedding shots may not be yours to use without obtaining the photographer's permission and/or paying a reuse fee.

Unless it's out of copyright, you may not scan printed fabric to make additional yardage, because the artwork belongs to the fabric company.

Even copyright-free imagery comes with guidelines specifying non-commercial usage and possibly limiting the number of images that may be used in a particular project. Some agreements require you to include credits if you use their images.

Standard copyright and terms of use agreements allow limited personal use for some images. Professional crafters may qualify for additional usage under a professional crafters policy, commonly called an "angel" policy, so check with the image provider for details.

Copyright laws can be complex. Visit the U.S. Copyright Office at www.copyright.gov for more information; if you didn't create a drawing, photograph or illustration, then you need permission to use it.

On CD-ROM

Many companies offer artwork on CD-ROM, either as individual images or complete collections. Image size, quality, copyright, usage agreements and system requirements vary among vendors, so read the fine print. Some companies offer images in multiple pre-determined sizes and formats, so getting the image off the CD-ROM and onto your fabric is as simple as selecting the size and file type you need and clicking "print." Other companies offer images in only a single size and format. You may need to alter the file in an editing program to get it to fit your needs.

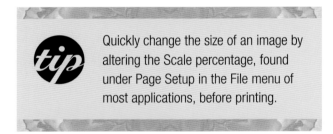

tip Quickly change the size of an image by altering the Scale percentage, found under Page Setup in the File menu of most applications, before printing.

Most CD-ROMs are 'read-only' and write-protected. Drag files to your hard drive, or open images in an editing program, and then save them to your hard drive or another disk to make changes.

You can usually search stock imagery by artist or photographer, subject matter, keyword or size. Fees vary, depending on the intended use and image quality. A high-resolution image suitable for commercial printing will cost more than a low-resolution image intended for a Web site or online newsletter. Stock houses charge per CD-ROM or per image.

10 oz. natural cotton duck fabric, Dharma Trading Co.

The Vintage Workshop clematis.jpg image and instructions for our Canvas Caddy bag are available on the CD-ROM.

Individual artists or groups of artists offer image collections on CD-ROMs. As with stock imagery, check the image size and quality, and pay extra attention to licensing restrictions. Some artists do not allow the sale of finished products created with their art, and others do not allow you to manipulate their work in any way. There may also be restrictions on using the images. For example, you may be allowed to print the image on paper or fabric, but digitizing the image for an embroidery motif, or printing gift wrap or stationery, etc., is prohibited.

For information about the imagery on the enclosed CD-ROM, see page 132.

Online

Many companies have Web sites where you can quickly search available imagery, preview usage agreements and file specifications, and purchase and download files immediately. Some companies also offer subscription-based options, in which you pay a flat fee for image access for a certain amount of time. Read agreements carefully for download restrictions and constraints.

Some companies are strictly shopping sites, while others offer additional perks and free downloads for prospective buyers to sample their wares. Magazines may offer online extras that correspond with projects featured in current print issues. Some items are online for a limited time, so download the images and archive them for future use.

In Print

Permission-free clip art books are available from a number of sources, and they may feature a variety of images, such as photos, illustrations and fine art images. Images can be copied or scanned directly from the pages, and some books include images on CD-ROM. Dover Publications, Search Press, Design Originals and Schiffer Publishing offer extensive clip art collections on a variety of subjects.

Don't overlook other image sources. Many scrapbooking, cardmaking and papercrafting products contain imagery that works well for fabric printing, too. Quilt label and design programs offer blocks, backgrounds, phrases, motifs and borders that can be printed quickly, providing "pieced" blocks in a fraction of the time.

It's an Original

Adding your own inspirations to your printed fabric makes any project that much more personal. Scan in your doodles, drawings and paintings, create a one-of-a-kind collage and edit your imagery any way you like. You won't have to worry about copyrights or usage agreements!

The Vintage Workshop Cotton Poplin

Printed Treasures Sew-On Fabric

Use your fabric printing skills to make teaching tools for children or those who may not do a task on a regular basis. These place mats show table-ware placement — silverware goes in the pocket, and plates and glasses belong on the place setting. Look for the silvware.jpg image and the project instructions on the CD-ROM.

Your child's original art — off the fridge and fresh from the printer — makes a memorable quilt.

It's a Snap

Capture creativity with a click! Digital cameras make it easy — and affordable — to get just the right image. In addition to the usual family fare of keepsake moments, consider creating your own personal archive of specialty shots. Grow a garden of digital flowers, take some trendy textures and look for landscapes in the viewfinder. Don't worry about any less-than-perfect pictures. Image-editing software offers ample opportunity to enhance your photos.

Import digital photos directly to your hard drive for editing and archiving, or print them immediately from all-in-one or photo printers that accept memory storage cards.

Don't despair if you haven't 'done digital' yet — many film processors can save your images to CD-ROM. Then, you can import and edit these images just as you would a digital shot.

Catching pets at their best can result in some fun shots. The eyeglass.jpg image and instructions for this simple spectacle case are on the CD-ROM.

(Eyes) Jacquard Products Silk; (Dogs) Jacquard Products Cotton, CK Ltd. photo

Scan-o-rama!

Perfect for capturing copies of flat media — your child's artwork, original photographs, doodles and drawings — the scanner can also be the means for creating your own unique images. Place items directly on the scanner bed to create collages. Layer objects for infinite effects. Combine photos, bits of paper, laces, trim and memorabilia. Scan sewing tools, candy, feathers, flowers, buttons, ribbons and trims, coins, sequins, sand, shells, hardware, bits of paper — the list is as endless as your imagination!

Before you begin, take a moment to familiarize yourself with your scanner's capabilities. Most scanners include stand-alone software or plug-ins for image-editing software. Functions vary between brands, models and software versions. Spending a few minutes to learn about your machine now can save you hours later. Read the manual or contact the manufacturer for information specific to your machine.

Remember, most scanners can operate with the lid open or closed, depending on the look you want for your art.

Buttons scanned with the lid closed.

Buttons scanned with no lid.

Scan It!

Check the scanner bed before placing anything on the glass. Make sure the surface is free of smudges, dust and other debris. Anything on the glass will be included in your scanned image. If you need to clean the scanner bed, check your manual for specific instructions. In general, you can use water or window cleaner to wipe the glass clean. Never spray anything directly on the glass, as any moisture inside the scanner could damage the machine. Instead, lightly spray a soft cloth and wipe the glass clean.

If you're working with wet or abrasive materials, like branches, fruit or sand, cover the scanner bed with clear acetate or acrylic film to protect it from scratches. Page protectors, cut to fit, work well.

Arrange items on the scanner bed as desired. Items closest to the glass will appear the most detailed in your scan, and those farther away will be less clear. If items are relatively flat, close the scanner lid before scanning. If items are dimensional or too delicate to support the weight of the scanner lid without being crushed, remove the lid

Textured or patterned fabrics and papers make interesting backgrounds for dimensional scans. Terrycloth, batik or metallic fabrics add another element to the scan. Crumpled tissue and textured paper create unique backgrounds.

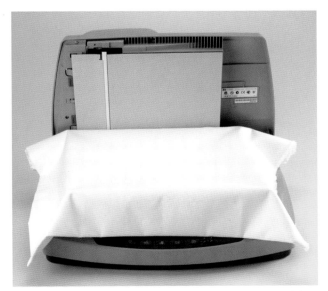

Carefully cover the foamboard box with fabric. Tuck fabric in around the edges to prevent exterior light from seeping in.

 Think inside the box!

Foamboard, available in office and art supply stores, is a lightweight foam laminated on both sides with coated-paper stock. You can cut it easily with a ruler and craft knife, and sections can be held together with tape or straight pins. Create a scanner box by cutting 3"-wide strips of foamboard a bit wider than the width and length of your scanner bed. Secure the corners together to make a box. Place it on the scanner bed and drape fabric across the top before scanning.

Create circular scanning rings easily by cutting a strip of flexible cardboard to the desired height, forming the strip into a circle and securing the ends together with tape.

or leave it in the raised position. Avoid unwanted backgrounds — and tedious digital "clean up" — by covering the items with fabric or a foamboard box. Try different backgrounds for various effects. The texture, color and pattern of the covering fabric will show in the scanned image if your items don't completely cover the scanner bed.

Plan your scan. Use a contrasting background to make it easier to outline your image in an editing program, or choose a background that will blend with the fabric in your project.

Save It

Images created on a copier must be printed directly to the fabric, because there is no way to store them, but scanned images can be saved to your computer hard drive. If you think you might want to use an image again, scan and save!

Scanned images can create large file sizes. Many file formats use compression to reduce file size. Lossless compression formats reduce the file without removing detail or color information. Lossy formats remove some detail in the file.

When possible, save files in an uncompressed file format that you can open in your image-editing or printing application. If your scanner is accessed from within an image-editing program, you can save your scan in that program's native format.

TIFF (Tagged Image File Format) is a standard file format accepted by almost all painting, image-editing and page-layout programs. It is a lossless format, which retains all the image information collected in the scan.

JPEG (Joint Photographic Experts Group) is a standard lossy file format, which allows you to save an image at a smaller file size. The amount of compression directly affects the image quality — higher compression equals lower quality and a lower file size. If you repeatedly resave an image in JPEG format, you'll lose data and detail each time.

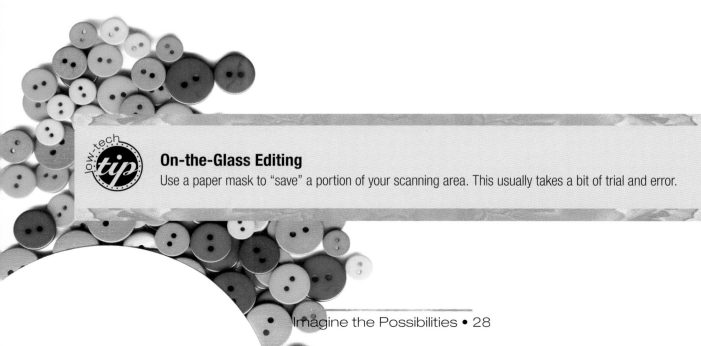

On-the-Glass Editing
Use a paper mask to "save" a portion of your scanning area. This usually takes a bit of trial and error.

Virtual Appliqué

At some point, almost every stitcher experiments with appliqué, a process in which one piece of fabric is stitched or applied to a second background fabric. While there are many traditional techniques, virtual appliqué offers a speedy advantage.

Create an appliquéd effect on the scanner bed by carefully layering items on the glass. Remember that you're working 'upside down,' so you must put the top items in place first. You may need to preview and adjust items several times before getting the desired result.

Another option is to create a clipping path, cutout or mask around appliqué items within your software program. Begin with digital images of both your appliqué item and a background image. Outline the image as desired, using either a clipping path or mask. Exact steps will vary, depending on which program you use. Layer images to achieve the look you want.

Image-editing programs make quick work of merging multiple images.

Text-ural Effects

Do not overlook the design possibilities of type and computer-generated characters. Even simple text offers many creative opportunities, either when used alone or incorporated with other imagery. Most computers come equipped with several different typefaces, and there are thousands of specialty fonts available. Basic text-editing or word processing programs allow you to change typeface, size, weight, format and color, giving you an infinite array of possibilities.

Fill an entire page with type for a background texture, or place text in various shapes to create interesting elements. If your software program doesn't allow you to fill shapes with text easily, create a block of text and use a mask to protect areas you don't want printed.

Use a simple word processing program to combine a poem or meaningful sonnet with an image. Just use the "insert image" command to bring in the design you need, and create a text box to add the words.

The Vintage Workshop Cotton Canvas

Words and symbols decorate this handy sewing tote. For project instructions, see the CD-ROM.

Blocks of text become interesting printed textures.

The Vintage Workshop Linen

Combine a slice of a imagery with a poem to create a personalized wedding keepsake. Fill in the appropriate names and date, and it becomes a one-of-a-kind gift that requires only a frame. The image, poem and project instructions are on the CD-ROM.

Button, Button...Who's got the button?

Veer off the beaten path by placing text along a new line.

Some software can be used to place text on a path. This makes it easy to create special effects with curves, swirls and zigzags of poetry, random thoughts or secret messages.

The Vintage Workshop, Asian Downloadable Collection/Chic Bag Boutique; The Vintage Workshop Linen; pattern: Indygo Junction Carry with Style

Copy or scan and print handwritten love letters or a child's scribbled message to add an unmistakably human touch to your printing. The Vintage Workshop has done the work for you with ready-made love note and postcard imagery.

Create interesting effects by layering several different type elements. Some programs allow you to create layers or stacks of imagery easily — or you can achieve a similar effect by reprinting different text elements on the same sheet of fabric. Overlapping letterforms, printed in different shades or colors, make unique textures and shapes.

Personalize almost any project by adding a name, clever saying, label or other word to an image or photo. Position the text to look like an integral part of the design.

Bubble Jet Set-treated cotton poplin

Put someone's name on this handy cosmetic bag, and there will never be a mix-up! The project instructions and cosmetic.jpg image are on the CD-ROM.

Image-editing Programs

Capturing images is just one of the first steps in creating a printed fabric project. Most likely, you'll want to tweak your work at some point — either by re-sizing a shot, cropping an image or eliminating that annoying 'red eye' effect. There are many image-editing programs available to help you do just that — and much, much more!

Features vary among programs, but most include these image optimization tools: re-size, rotate, flip, crop, color adjustment, levels, brightness/contrast, hue/saturation and sharpen. Some also have image repair tools, such as clone or retouch, dodge/burn, and advanced color correction.

With so many options available, how do you choose? While you're searching for the perfect software solution, keep these issues in mind:

Cost

In addition to the program cost, consider any software or hardware upgrades you might need to purchase to run the program on your computer. Read the system requirements and compare them with your machine. Does the program include a manual or help files, or will you need to buy a third-party guide and/or invest in training courses? What about program upgrades? Will it be necessary to 'stay current' when a newer version comes out? Is technical support available? If so, what is the cost?

The Learning Curve

Some programs are very intuitive. Others will require you to spend some time learning how to use the software. If possible, 'test drive' the program you're considering before you buy it. Many software publishers offer downloadable demo or evaluation versions of their products. Check company Web sites to see what is available. Research forums or newsgroups for users' opinions of the product.

Longevity

Don't overlook the importance of purchasing from an established company. If you run into a problem, you don't want to discover that the software manufacturer has gone out of business. Consider how long a program has been on the market, how often new versions are released and whether or not tech support, online tutorials, user forums, blogs or galleries are available.

Features

With so many features to choose from, it may help to work backwards. Ask yourself what you want to do with the software, and then compare your 'wish list' with the program's feature list. Check the program's ability to open and import the file format your scanner or camera provides.

Popular Programs

Note: This information was current when written. Check manufacturers' Web sites for the latest software developments.

Adobe Photoshop
www.adobe.com

Available for Mac and Windows.

Long considered an industry standard by imaging professionals, Adobe Photoshop is packed with optimization and repair tools, filters and special effects. There is little Photoshop cannot do with images, and the program's high price reflects its sophistication. The learning curve can be fairly steep, but online help files will get you started. The Adobe Web site is packed with tutorials, training options and user forums. Third-party plug-ins, add-ons and training materials are available as well.

Adobe Photoshop Elements
www.adobe.com

Available for Mac and Windows.

If the full version of Photoshop is more muscle than you need, consider Photoshop Elements. The scaled-down version of Adobe's image-editing program contains many of the most popular features of the full version, plus fun effects to artistically enhance your images. Photoshop Elements packs plenty of pixel-pushing power, and it is much more affordable for most home users.

Corel Paint Shop Pro
http://www.corel.com/

Available for Windows.

Corel Paint Shop Pro offers professional-looking results at an affordable price. Quickly adjust and retouch images using standard settings, or click for more advanced options. Create quick collages or add creative touches with filters and special effects. An easy-to-use learning center guides users to the right tool for the task at hand. Organize and share images with the included Corel Photo Album software.

Microsoft Digital Image Suite
www.microsoft.com

Available for Windows.

Microsoft offers several versions of its Digital Image Suite. Each version features simple image optimization, one-click color correction and auto-fix options, plus an interface for organizing images quickly. Though not as robust as Elements, Digital Image Suite is easy to use. The Standard package offers the most basic set of tools, while the Suite includes more image-editing options and specialty features. The Suite Plus package has video options as well.

Some computers, digital cameras, scanners and printers include basic photo-editing software. Don't overlook the features in these 'freebie' programs. They're often easy-to-learn and do just what you want — and the price is right!

Specialty Software

If these programs don't satisfy your digital desires, you may want to look into third-party plug-ins or specialty programs. Plug-ins are software modules that add capabilities to the host program and provide solutions for specific tasks. Software manufacturers usually provide plug-in listings or links on their product Web site. Specialty programs are stand-alone applications geared toward accomplishing a very specific task instead of providing an all-encompassing product answer. Here are just a few:

Electric Quilt 5 (EQ5)
www.electricquilt.com

Available for Windows.

For a full-featured quilt design program, you can't beat Electric Quilt 5. Packed with features, EQ5 is fun and user-friendly. The program comes with libraries of pre-designed blocks, fabrics and layouts; also, you can import your own fabrics, modify or draw your own blocks and save your original quilt designs. EQ5 takes the guesswork out of fabric estimating by providing rotary cutting charts and yardage requirements. You can print foundation patterns, appliqué templates and note cards as well.

Kaleidoscope Collections, LLC's Kaleidoscope Kreator
www.KalCollections.com

Available for Windows.

Originally created with scrapbooking in mind, Kaleidoscope Kreator's unique images provide an artistic option for printed fabric projects. Original images are transformed into kaleidoscope-like creations in four easy steps — just open, position, preview and print. Import your own files, or use one of the more than 100 high-quality photos included on the CD-ROM. Choose from twelve kaleidoscope shapes, re-size, rotate, flip and move images in the wedge-shaped work space, and then preview before printing or saving. Edit saved files in other image-editing programs.

Genuine Fractals
www.ononesoftware.com

Available for Mac and Windows. Requires Adobe Photoshop.

Is your image looking a little rough when enlarged? Genuine Fractals may be just what you need. You can scale images up to 800% with no degradation. This program is quite affordable if you have a lot of images to enlarge.

Quiltsmart Photo Shapes
www.quiltsmart.com

Available for Mac and Windows.

Designed to duplicate the look of a double wedding ring quilt, this program works with the Hewlett-Packard Label program and allows you to import family photos into the quilt arc patterns.

Quiltsmart Photo Shapes

CHAPTER 3
FINDING FABRIC

Anything you can print on paper, you can print on fabric. But what kind of fabric should you use, and where do you find it?

Finding Fabric

Choosing fabric is a fun part of the printing process. However, there are some limitations. You must use a natural fiber fabric so the ink will permanently penetrate the fibers. Cotton or silk works best, but you can also print on lightweight wool, linen and some rayons. Ink will not adhere to synthetic fabrics permanently, so the image will fade or wash out.

There are many brands of ready-to-print fabrics available — or you can prepare your own. Ready-to-print fabrics offer immediate results. You just open the package and print! Preparing your own fabrics is more cost-effective and offers more flexibility because you aren't as limited in fabric choices, but it does take time and testing to learn which methods work best.

 tip If you absolutely must print on a synthetic material, consider image transfers. In this process, you print an image on a special release paper, and then heat press or transfer the image to a synthetic material. Most transfer products change the hand or feel of the fabric.

Ready-to-print

Most fabric, quilting and craft stores carry 8 ½" x 11" sheets of ready-to-print fabrics. Depending on the brand, there are usually three to 10 sheets of white or off-white cotton, linen or silk fabric in each package. Common cotton fabric options include satin, twill, poplin, canvas, denim, broadcloth, lawn, sheeting and muslin. Silk options include habotai, charmeuse, organza, satin, crepe and chiffon. The fabric is chemically pre-treated with an ink fixative and adhered to a carrier that will feed the fabric through the printer. Some brands offer self-adhesive or fusible fabric options.

8 ½" x 14", 11" x 17" and 13" x 19" sheets of prepared fabric are available, along with RTP (ready-to-print) fabrics on a roll for banner or large-scale printing. Color Textiles offers kits with pre-cut bias silk for neckties, scarves and other items. Some companies offer sampler packs containing one or

Quickly print a scarf, table runner or banner using ready-to-print fabrics on a roll.

more sheets of several fabric types. Try various brands and fabric types to see which ones you (and your printer) like best for a particular project.

Read all instructions carefully while working with ready-to-print products. Different brands have different directions. Some products require post-printing rinsing or heat-setting. Most RTP manufacturers recommend that you let the printed piece "cure" before washing or working with the fabric. Fabric prepared for scrapbooking may not be treated to hold the ink, because it isn't meant to be washed.

Store ready-to-print fabric according to the manufacturer's instructions — usually in its original plastic bag at room temperature in a low-humidity environment. Never store treated fabric — either ready-to-print or fabric you've prepared yourself — in direct sunlight. Store fabric sheets flat to avoid possible printing problems.

Make instant appliqués with fusible or adhesive-backed ready-to-print fabrics.

tip Panorama photos are great for printing on ties!

Special Effects

Check out your favorite store for specialty ready-to-print fabrics. Some companies make self-adhesive versions and fusible sheets — both are perfect for crafts or when it isn't necessary to sew the fabric to the base. These can often be combined with sewable versions in the same or coordinating projects.

Look for June Tailor laser-cut fabric frames to showcase your favorite photos. The intricate cutting work is done for you; just iron it on. Onlookers will be amazed at your handiwork! A special downloadable program ensures perfect positioning.

Fabric paper — a very stiff fabric used for scrapbooking and papercrafting — can be used without any stabilizer, because the stiffness will carry it through the printer. However, this specialty fabric isn't pre-treated and cannot be washed.

June Tailor You've Been Framed; Melissa A. Livesey photo

June Tailor Quick Fuse fabric, CD-ROM image coneflower.jpg

Personalize a portfolio or other office gear with fusible ready-to-print fabric. Project instructions and the flower image are available on the CD-ROM.

The Vintage Workshop has Gloss Finish Artist Canvas for creating your own art reproductions, framed prints, etc. Apply a clear fixative after printing for added durability.

Jacquard Products offers ready-to-print ExtravOrganza. Use this for scrapbooking or creating artistic effects with sheer overlays and just a hint of color.

Some ready-to print fabrics may shrink during the post-printing treatment recommended by the manufacturer. Where applicable, print extra imagery to account for the discrepancy, or be flexible with your finished project size.

Create decorating items with ready-to-print canvas.

Sheer fabric makes wonderful sachet holders, and this simple drawstring bag can have many other uses as well. Find the kaleidoscope image and the project instructions on the enclosed CD-ROM.

Preparing Your Own Fabric

Preparing your own printable fabric opens up a world of possibilities, because you are not limited to manufacturer's pre-packaged choices anymore. Whatever you're willing to put through your printer is fair game!

Choosing Fabric

As mentioned previously, natural fibers are a must for making permanent washable images. Look for 100-percent cotton, linen or silk fabrics.

The weave of the fabric will determine the clarity of your printed image. Smooth, tightly woven fabric shows the best detail, but using textured cloth can produce interesting effects.

For near photographic printing, look for 200-count cotton fabric. Thread count refers to the number of threads within a square inch of fabric. Check fabric bolt ends for content and thread count information. Examine both the right and wrong sides of the fabric. The weave may appear smoother on one side than on the other.

White fabric best portrays accurate skin tones.

Printed Treasures Sew-On Fabric; BJS treated fabric

A smooth surface texture allows fabric to feed through the printer easily and promotes an even distribution of ink. Any novelty, raised area or decorative weave can result in uneven ink placement — and interesting results.

Pre-printed fabrics, such as white-on-white cottons, mottled textures or batiks also create intriguing effects. Remember, there is no white ink in inkjet printers, and inks are not opaque. The fabric color will show through, and dark fabric colors may overpower your printed image. Textures, stripes and dots can create some unique effects, though family members printed on polka dots can look like they have the measles.

White fabric is your best bet for reproducing color images, while off-white tones lend an heirloom appearance to your prints. Light- and mid-tone fabrics work well for most projects.

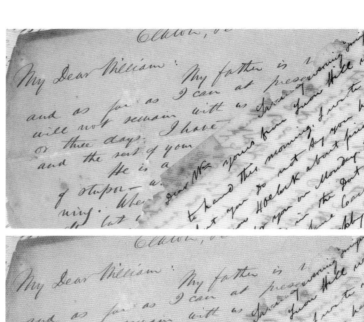
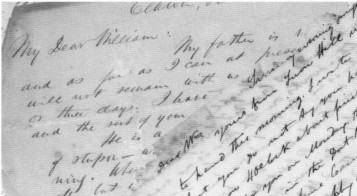
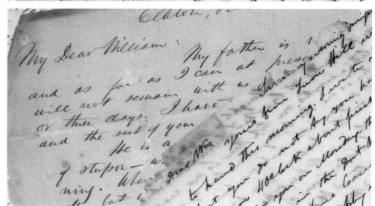

Top to bottom: Electric Quilt Cotton Satin, The Vintage Workshop Cotton Canvas and The Vintage Workshop Linen; CD-ROM image ScrapSmart letters.jpg

The finer the weave, the more detail your image will have.

Simple Steps

Using Bubble Jet Set 2000 (BJS), an ink fixative, you can prepare fabric for printing with four simple steps:

1. Pre-wash
2. Rough cut
3. Soak
4. Stabilize

Pre-wash

Pre-washing your fabric helps remove any factory finishes that might inhibit fibers from absorbing the chemical fixative. You may want to hand wash delicate silk, lace or netting. Sturdier cotton and canvas fabrics can handle machine washing.

Bubble Jet Rinse (also used for post-treating printed fabric) is a good choice for pre-washing fabric you plan to soak in BJS 2000. Partially fill the washing machine with cold water and add ½ cup of Bubble Jet Rinse. Add your fabric, and let the machine cycle as usual. Tumble or line dry. Iron while the fabric is still slightly damp. Do not use steam.

Note: To pre-shrink cotton fabrics, machine wash and tumble dry.

Synthrapol, made by Jacquard Products, can be used as a pre-wash instead of Bubble Jet Rinse. Many textile artists use Synthrapol as a pre-wash and post-treatment for paint and dye work. Add three tablespoons of Synthrapol plus two tablespoons of soda ash per eight pound machine load. Use hot water.

Bubble Jet Set 2000, manufactured by C. Jenkins Co., is the most commonly-used fixative on the market and produces excellent results. Chemicals in the BJS solution help bind ink to fabric. One 32-ounce bottle will prepare 40 to 50 letter-sized pieces of fabric, depending on fabric weight and density.

C. Jenkins also offers Bubble Jet Rinse for pre- and post-printing care.

Soft Fabric Photos offers an alternative kit (using Jacquard Products Dyeset Concentrate) for making your own fabric sheets.

Rough Cut

Cut fabric slightly larger than the size of your printed piece. For an 8 ½" x 11" print, cut fabric about 9" x 12". Rough cutting fabric slightly larger than the final print makes it easier to apply the stabilizer.

To prepare several sheets of fabric, cut strips slightly larger than the size of one dimension of your final printed piece by the width of your yardage. If necessary, use paper templates of the finished print size to figure out how to get the most from your yardage.

The width and length of your printed piece will depend on your project, printer capabilities and image. Some printer and software combinations can print banners and other custom sizes, allowing you to print lengths of 50" or more.

Note: If your fabric contains a pattern, print or distinctive weave, take this into consideration before cutting. A striped fabric printed off-grain will always be off-grain.

Soak

You'll need a flat plastic container to soak your fabric. Choose a container with a flat bottom — no large ridges or bumps — that is 3" to 4" deep. The container should be large enough that a single sheet of rough cut fabric will lie flat in the bottom, but small enough that you won't need a lot of liquid to immerse the material. Clear plastic totes, storage boxes or even unused cat litter trays work well.

Safety first! Work in a well-ventilated area, and wear rubber gloves while dealing with the chemical solution. Follow manufacturer's directions carefully.

Place one sheet of rough-cut fabric flat in the bottom of the container. Shake the BJS, and pour a small amount of the solution onto the fabric. Gently work the solution into the fabric with your fingers, adding

more liquid as needed. The BJS solution reacts to oxygen, so it's best to use only as much as needed for each project.

If you rough cut your fabric into single sheets, layer additional sheets on top of the first, working the solution into each one and adding more BJS as needed. Rub out any air bubbles, because they will prevent the solution from penetrating the fabric. If you rough cut your fabric into strips, lay one end of the strip in the container, work the solution into it, then work your way up the rest of the strip, accordion-folding the fabric and adding solution as needed. You should end up with a well-soaked stack of fabric without a lot of excess solution in the bottom of your container.

Let the fabric soak in the solution for five minutes, and then let it air dry, either by laying the fabric flat on a towel or hanging it to dry. Do not wring fabric. If you hang the fabric outside to dry, keep it out of direct sunlight. Avoid draping fabric in a way that could cause an uneven distribution of the BJS solution. Save any liquid solution left in the container in a tightly capped bottle. Keep used solution separate from fresh BJS to avoid contaminating the chemical.

Note: BJS has a one-year shelf life after the bottle has been opened. Store BJS liquid out of direct sunlight. The solution will oxidize, or lose strength when exposed to air. If you can't use BJS-treated fabric right away, seal it in an airtight plastic bag and store out of the sun in a cool, dry place. Test-print treated fabric that has been stored for any length of time.

Stabilize

Before you can print on your prepared fabric, you must adhere it to a temporary backing that will carry it through the printer. Except for heavy-weight canvas or stiff scrapbooking fabric papers, fabric alone is too flimsy to feed through a printer. A backing gives the printer something solid to grip and keeps the fabric from shifting while it travels under the printhead. A backing also acts as a barrier, protecting your printer from extra ink that might otherwise be left in the print path if you're printing on a lightweight or openweave material. Wait until you're ready to print to apply fabric to the backing, or the two materials may pull apart over time.

Iron your fabric before adhering it to any backing. Use a dry iron (not steam), and work on a firm — not padded — ironing surface. Steam can cause water spots that will interfere with printing. Cloth-covered plywood or particle board works well for a firm surface. Iron both sides of the fabric if necessary, taking care not to scorch the material.

There are several options for backing materials. Experiment to find what works best for you.

When placing backings onto treated fabric, pay attention to lengthwise and crosswise grain. Grainlines cannot be adjusted after printing.

Freezer Paper

Freezer paper is available in most grocery or art supply stores. Sold on a roll in the paper products or plastic storage bag section, freezer paper has a thin plastic or wax coating on one side. By ironing the shiny-coated side to your fabric, you can create a backing for your fabric quickly and easily.

To apply freezer paper to prepared fabric, center the paper, shiny side down, on the wrong side of the fabric. Start in the middle, and press slowly toward the outer edges with a dry iron. Heat from the iron will soften the coating on the shiny side of the paper just enough to let it temporarily adhere to the fabric. Make sure all edges are firmly adhered and there are no air bubbles or wrinkles. Turn the fabric over and iron from the right side if necessary.

Some companies make a heavier weight freezer paper in pre-cut sizes. This paper has extra adhesion and works well for fabric printing.

Self-adhesive Labels

Full-sheet (8 ½" x 11") re-positionable adhesive labels, available at office supply stores, are quick and easy re-usable stabilizers. Most labels have a split paper backing. Peel off a portion of the backing, and smooth the label into place on the wrong side of the fabric. Smooth away any air bubbles or wrinkles, and make sure the edges are secure. Do not iron fabric while the label is attached. Save the paper backing. After printing, labels can be removed from the printed piece and used again.

Standard Paper or Cardstock

Temporary spray adhesive and ordinary paper or cardstock work well as fabric backings. There are many adhesive sprays on the market. Steer clear of those with permanent bonds and those not intended for fabric or paper. Follow manufacturer's directions, and always work in a well-ventilated area. When possible, spray outside, using a cardboard box or large plastic trash bag to protect any surfaces and catch overspray.

Lightly spray the paper or cardstock. Let the spray dry slightly, so that the paper is tacky but not wet when applied to the fabric. Hold the sprayed backing by one corner, and starting at the opposite corner, smooth the backing onto the wrong side of your treated fabric. If necessary, use a brayer to burnish away air bubbles, or peel and re-apply the backing to eliminate wrinkles. Make sure all of the edges are secure.

Fusible Web

If you plan to appliqué your printed image onto another surface, save yourself a step by using paper-backed fusible web as a stabilizer. Following manufacturer's directions, iron the fusible web to the wrong side of fabric, but do NOT remove the protective paper backing on the opposite side. Be sure the paper backing is firmly attached before printing the fabric. Once the fabric is printed, trim the image, remove the protective paper and fuse as directed.

Clogged nozzles can spit big globs of glue onto your backing, leaving stains on the fabric.

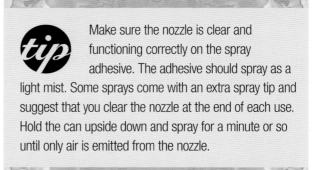

tip Make sure the nozzle is clear and functioning correctly on the spray adhesive. The adhesive should spray as a light mist. Some sprays come with an extra spray tip and suggest that you clear the nozzle at the end of each use. Hold the can upside down and spray for a minute or so until only air is emitted from the nozzle.

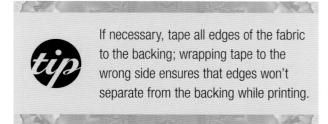

Apply a piece of masking tape to the leading edge of the backing if your printer has trouble picking up the fabric sheet. This extra bit of stiffness sometimes helps the fabric feed through.

Embroidery Stabilizers

Machine embroidery stabilizers can also be used as backings for printed fabrics. Choose a sturdy, temporary iron-on version, or use a temporary spray adhesive to attach the stabilizer to the wrong side of the treated fabric. Pay close attention to edges. It may be necessary to tape the edges to hold them securely. Embroidery stabilizer is relatively expensive, but it can be reused for its intended purpose after printing.

After you've applied your backing, trim excess fabric from the edges using a rotary cutter and ruler. If you're using a pre-cut backing, use the backing edges as a trim guide. To make it easier to remove the backing later, leave a short length of fabric extending past the backing's lower edge. This extra length serves as a handle to remove the stabilizer after printing.

You're ready to print!

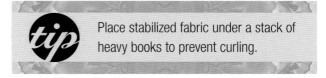
Clip a tiny triangle off both leading edge corners to prevent printer mis-feeds and help the leading edge of the fabric sheet feed into the printer.

CHAPTER 4
PRINTING 101

You've found the perfect image and prepared the fabric. You're ready to print! Do you have everything you need?

Before you press that print button, assemble these just-in-case items. You don't want to be digging around in your desk for a tool while your fabric wrinkles and jams in the printer.

- Long-handled tweezers to tame curling edges and eliminate printer jams.

- Letter opener or flat knife for guiding printed fabric past the last set of paper grabbers (or pizza wheels) as it exits the printer.

- Brayer or old rolling pin to make sure the backing is firmly adhered to the fabric.

- Sharp scissors for clipping — not pulling — raveling threads.

- Lint roller for eliminating stray threads and pet hair from your fabric. Be careful — some rollers are extra tacky, and they can actually pull your fabric away from the backing. A piece of masking tape wrapped around your fingers works well too.

- Rotary cutter, ruler and mat for last minute trims.

If you're not familiar with your printer already, take a good look at it now. How does the paper feed through? Which side is "up" in the paper tray? Can you cancel print jobs? If necessary, review your printer manual for information. Make sure the paper tray and path are clean and clear of ink overspray, lint and dust. If necessary, clean the outside of your printer with a damp cloth. Use a soft brush, cotton swab or vacuum cleaner to remove lint and dirt from the paper path. Follow manufacturer's directions to clean ink cartridges or printheads.

Can You Cancel?

If you notice a misfeed or paper jam in the making, you may be able to salvage the print — or at least avoid a severe jam — by interrupting or canceling printing. Generally, you can cancel printing by pressing a button, lifting the printer cover or selecting an option in the print queue. Check your printer to see which options are available.

If all else fails, turn the printer off to cancel printing.

Which Way is Up?

Most printers include some sort of symbol to indicate how to place paper in the tray. Look for a symbol in the plastic of the paper path. You can also mark a piece of paper, take note of how you placed it in the tray and test-print to determine if you should place your fabric face up or face down.

Watch how the paper travels through the printer. Some printers pick up the page, curl it around a roller and print on the underside while feeding it through. Others print on the upper side of the paper while the paper travels straight through and out the opposite side of the machine. Straight feed is sometimes available as a manual feed option. Check your printer information for available options.

CD-ROM image dogfrmft.jpg

Got Ink?

Check the ink level in your cartridges before printing. Some manufacturers include tools for estimating ink levels, testing, cleaning and calibrating printers with their print driver installations. You don't want to run out of ink in the midst of a large print job. Waning stripes and off-color lines are hard to disguise in the final project.

If you're planning to print a lot of fabric, consider installing a fresh ink cartridge. Most printers allow you to remove a partially-used cartridge, insert a new one, and then re-insert the old cartridge later on. Store partially-used cartridges in an air-tight plastic bag. Protect the printhead from drying out by re-applying the protective coverings that come with new cartridges.

Kaleidoscope Kutz image

Running out of ink will cause a gradual loss of color or stripes.

Take Time to Test Print

Print your image on paper the same size as your fabric sheet. Check image size and placement, and if you're grouping multiple images on a page, make sure each image has adequate seam allowances all the way around. Depending on the project, you'll need a ¼" to ½" seam allowance around each image. If you intend to fuse the images, a ⅛" allowance should suffice. If you're using a borderless or full-bleed printer, such as a photo printer that prints to the edge of the paper or fabric, you may need to adjust margins to accommodate seam allowance needs. If necessary, make adjustments and re-test before printing on fabric.

Don't waste valuable treated fabric — print multiple images on a page if space allows, but remember that seam allowances are needed for adjoining images. Small slivers of designs can be used for bookmarks, covering buttons, scrapbook accents, etc.

This simple but oh-so-practical shoe bag is perfect for traveling or organizing special shoes in your closet. Use the instructions and the blueshoe.jpg on the CD-ROM, or substitute a photo of your own shoes.

June Tailor Quick Fuse

Cheap Tricks

When test printing, save ink by setting your printer to "draft" or "fast" mode. You also may be able to decrease ink volume and select Grayscale to use only your black cartridge. Look for paper type and quality settings under print options to see what is available.

You may want to test print on an extra piece of fabric before plunging into a new project.

Make sure your hands are clean before handling fabric. Dirt and oil transfer easily, and both can interfere with print quality!

Before printing, make sure the backing is adhered to the fabric securely, and check the fabric sheet for wrinkles or air bubbles. Use masking tape or a lint roller to remove any debris from the fabric surface. Trim wayward strands of fabric from all edges of the fabric sheet. Loose threads can get caught in the printer mechanism. Be sure the fabric sheet is flat. Press curled edges with a dry iron.

Remove all paper from the printer feed tray. Place one sheet of fabric in the tray, being careful to place the fabric right side up or down as required for your printer. Some ready-to-print fabrics have printed backing sheets, which help you determine which side should be placed up in the tray. Do not stack printable fabric sheets. Align the fabric sheet with printer paper guides, making sure it is square against the feeding mechanism. If the fabric feeds in at an angle, the printer may jam or misprint the image on the page. It's important that the fabric feeds through the printer straight and flat — if not, your image will not print properly.

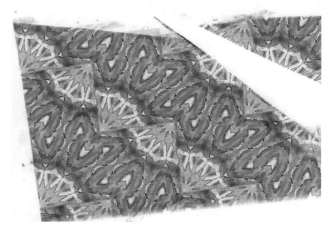

Kaleidoscope Kutz image

A misfed sheet can be harvested for usable sections.

Anything left on the fabric surface will act as a resist and leave an unprinted area on the fabric.

Printer properties include a host of options for paper type (or fabric weight), ink volume, printing quality, etc. Adjust printer settings to "Normal" or "Best" quality, and set ink volume to the default. A plain paper setting works for most fabrics. If your fabric is thicker than cotton broadcloth or muslin, try a thick, plain paper, card stock or matte paper setting. Setting options vary from printer to printer, so it's a good idea to jot down test print selections and results.

Maximize fabric by printing multiple tests on one sheet of fabric. Test print small images by placing them at one end or in a corner of the page. Print your next test image in the open area by feeding the opposite end of the page through the printer first.

Record Breaking

Keep a notebook of printed samples and document your results. Include test swatches, and label each swatch with the fabric type, image used, and pertinent software or printer settings. Jot down any extra information that might be helpful later. Date each entry, and store the notebook as you would the finished print — safely out of direct sunlight. Your notebook will become a handy reference for refreshing your memory or planning your next printed project.

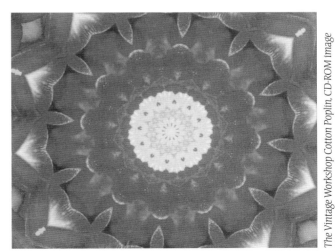

The Vintage Workshop Cotton Poplin, CD-ROM image kkcrocus.jpg

Notice the difference in clarity between the draft (right) and best quality (left) settings.

Let the printer pick up and feed the fabric at its own pace. Don't push it into the machine or try to hurry it along. When "best" quality settings are selected, more ink is applied to the print than in "normal" or "draft" modes. Extra drying time is added to the print job so the image doesn't smear when it emerges from the printer.

The fabric should feed through the printer just like paper. If the printer doesn't pick up the fabric sheet or you get an error message, check to make sure the fabric is flat. Clip corners ¼" diagonally on the leading edge. Make sure the backing is still adhered securely, and try again.

If you have trouble with the leading edge of your fabric separating from the backing sheet, tape along the leading edge of the fabric sheet, wrapping the tape over to the back. The tape should not extend into the printing area.

Enclose the leading edge of the fabric with tape.

Printer Jam Prevention

Listen to your printer. Just as that light rattle in the bobbin case of your sewing machine tells you that you're running out of thread, you'll soon be able to hear the slightest sound of a misfeed or other problem.

It's best to be nearby while printing fabric. Early intervention may save a misprint. On most printers, you can watch the paper or fabric feed into the machine. Pay attention to the leading edge as it feeds through the rollers and paper guides. The paper grabbers or "pizza wheels" may inadvertently separate the fabric from its backing. Depending on your printer, you may be able to prevent a jam by gently grabbing the leading edge of the fabric with long-handled tweezers and guiding it past the wheels, or by using a slim knife or letter opener to help feed the front edge under the wheels. Do not pull or yank on the fabric, because it will likely distort the image and cause a jam. Be careful to steer clear of the print cartridge path, and do not insert anything directly under the wheels. These actions could damage your printer.

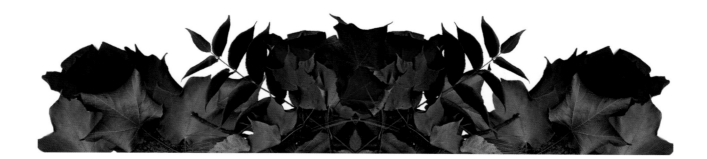

Your printed fabric images may not look as bright or detailed as they do on screen, because the fabric fibers are absorbing the ink — imagine a paper towel or sponge soaking up a spill. You may need to increase the color saturation settings in your print properties or image-editing program in order to replicate the intense color you see onscreen. Adjust the ink volume settings if your print appears dull or washed out.

Just as quality varies among printers, images will look different on different fabrics. Rough weaves and canvases won't appear as detailed as smooth cotton prints. On thin, light fabrics like silk, images may show through to the back of the fabric when printed at "best" quality. This may be desirable for certain projects, like scarves, where both sides of the fabric will show; but you may want to use the "normal" setting to prevent too much ink from blurring images on other projects.

Make sure your printed fabric is completely dry before handling. Let it sit several minutes. Check manufacturer's suggestions, and if necessary for your climate, wait longer. Some artists suggest waiting 24 hours (other say more than a week) before rinsing and using fabric prints. Allowing the ink to "cure" helps images retain more depth, brightness and saturation. Keep prints out of direct sunlight while curing. Handle printed sheets around the edges, not on the printed image.

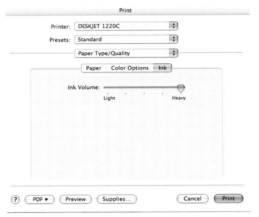

Increase ink volume to intensify color.

After the waiting period, gently remove the backing from the fabric. Support the fabric while the backing is peeled away, being careful not to distort the image and fabric weave. If you backed your fabric with fusible web, remove only the protective paper, not the web.

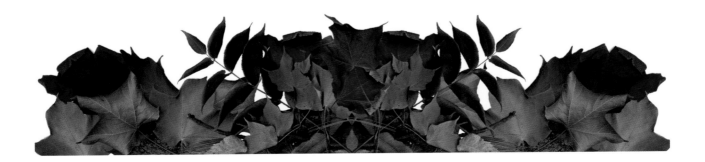

Post Printing

Follow manufacturer's directions for post-printing treatments. Some require rinsing, while others recommend heat-setting with a dry iron. Do not use steam, because water spots could mar the image.

Rinse

Rinsing the printed image removes any non-absorbed ink from your fabric that could bleed to surrounding fabrics later. Use enough water and recommended rinsing agent so the displaced ink will not reattach to your print. Some fabrics may shrink during the rinsing process.

To rinse images, use a plastic tub large enough for the print to lie flat without folding in on itself. For fabric prepared with Bubble Jet Set 2000, use two

Ink in the rinse water gave these prints an unintended tea-dyed look.

ounces of Bubble Jet Rinse per gallon of water. For most printings, you'll likely need to start with a minimum of two gallons of water and four ounces of Rinse.

Rinse each print individually for at least two minutes. Immerse fabric in water, gently moving it back and forth and side to side beneath the water surface. Do not allow fabric to fold over on itself, as ink could transfer from one surface to another. You may see a plume of ink in the water when the fabric is first submerged. This is the non-absorbed ink floating away from the fabric. By keeping the fabric moving, you prevent the ink from re-attaching to the fabric. Don't lift the fabric up and down out of the water. This will exaggerate ink runs and blur your image.

Change the rinse solution when the water becomes colored. Ink suspended in the rinse water could attach to light areas of other prints, and your prints could take on a tinted look.

Dry

Lay rinsed prints flat to air dry on an absorbent towel. Do not twist, wring or stack wet prints. Laying prints flat helps reduce the chance of ink runs and bleeding. It's best to wait until images are thoroughly dry before ironing, because pressing wet images with a dry iron can degrade results.

Caring for Your Printed Images

Repeated washings will eventually fade printed images — think of what happens to denim jeans or manufactured fabrics that are washed repeatedly. Washing can yield a mellow, aged look, but you may not really want that.

Instead, you may use a screen and handheld vacuum to remove any dust from your project.

If you must wash your printed fabric project, use a gentle detergent with cool or cold water and the delicate wash cycle. Better yet, hand wash your project in a sink or tub, making sure that the wet fabric doesn't fold in on itself and transfer ink. Dry garments flat.

tip

Try this test: Print two images. Store one in a light-safe place, and subject the other to the rigors of washing, dry cleaning and sunlight. Wait a week, a month or more. Then compare results.

Kaleidoscope images and project instructions are on the CD-ROM.

Kaleidoscope Kutz kksilk.jpg on the CD-ROM

CHAPTER 5
BEYOND THE BASICS

Now that you've mastered basic fabric prep and printing, it won't be long before the "What if … ?" bug bites you, too. Try these alteration techniques to enhance your images and expand your knowledge of inkjet fabric printing.

Hibiscus.jpg image on the CD-ROM

Original image

The possibilities for variations on a single image are endless. These alterations were all done using a very simple graphics program and the hibiscus.jpg image on the CD-ROM.

Negative Color

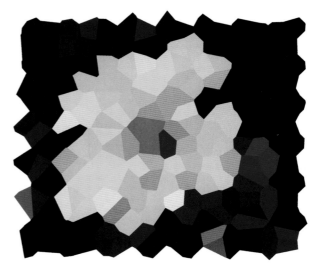

Mosaic

Pencil Sketch

Charcoal Contrast

Color Change

Glow Edges

Transparent Fade

Photocopy

Vertical Waves

Pointillist

Faded Crisscross

Altering Imagery

Altered images are all the rage. Amateurs and professional artists alike can't resist tweaking, tearing or totally transforming images. Anything goes when creating altered images, and inkjet printed fabric is a perfect medium for playing with some of these wonderful techniques.

Although every altered image is unique, using the same techniques can produce many different pictures. Some images are the result of using an image-editing program, while others may be replicated with our low-tech tips!

Don't be afraid to explore extra features and filters in your editing software. Select "File … Save As", and rename your digital image to make a copy, so you'll always have the original intact. Worried you won't like an effect? In most cases, alterations can be reversed with a simple "Edit — Undo" command — or you can close a file without saving it.

Image-editing software is faster and more user-friendly than ever. Techniques that used to be quite complicated now require just a few clicks of the mouse. Some techniques are even included as easy-to-apply menu choices on all-in-one machines. It doesn't get much simpler than that!

Most image-editing programs allow you to flip, flop, rotate and reflect images to create complex-looking designs. Flop or reflect images vertically or horizontally for mirrored effects. Any text in the image will appear backward in the finished print. This is handy for creating iron-on transfers or secret messages that can be read in the mirror.

Rotate and repeat images to create unique designs. Some programs are limited to 45-degree or 90-degree angles, while others allow you to set specific increments.

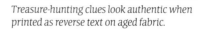

The Vintage Workshop Linen; Miss Mary's Quaint & Curious Clip Art

Treasure-hunting clues look authentic when printed as reverse text on aged fabric.

June Tailor Colorfast Sew-In Inkjet Fabric Sheets; CD-ROM image coneflower.jpg

Turn, turn, turn an image into a personalized design.

Scanner software often includes image correction tools that allow you to alter the resulting scan. Common tools allow you to make white and black point settings, tonal curve adjustments, brightness and contrast changes, and other color corrections. Some software also includes filters that can descreen pre-printed materials to avoid moirés, restore faded photographs, automatically remove dust, scratches and folds from images, or apply other special effects. Depending on your scanner's capabilities, some or all of the following functions may be available. Check your scanner software to see what options are available.

Crop images to emphasize important areas or eliminate unwanted elements.

Design Originals image, Vintage Ephemera, 7D-5242

Maintain proportions while re-sizing images, or distort them for artistic effects.

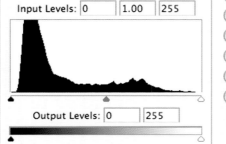

Levels

Channel: Gray

Input Levels: 0 | 1.00 | 255

Output Levels: 0 | 255

OK
Cancel
Load...
Save...
Auto
Options...

☑ Preview

Adjust white and black point settings to define highlights and shadows, and enhance detail in very light and dark image areas. Set the white point to define the lightest highlights and the black point to define the deepest shadows in an image. The rest of the image will be adjusted according to the settings.

The tonal curve represents contrast in a grayscale or color image. Drag points along the curve to lighten or darken specific tonal areas in an image. In general, the upper portion of the curve affects the lighter areas of an image, while the lower part affects darker areas. Change tones in the overall image, or select a specific color channel to alter. Careful! Minute shifts can create large changes in the image.

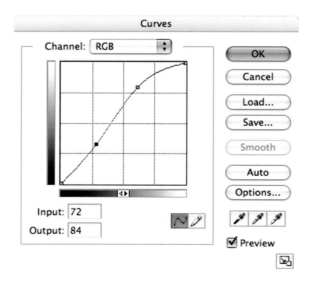

Increasing or decreasing brightness in an image affects all its tones. Increase brightness to lighten an image, or decrease brightness if an image looks "washed out."

Contrast refers to the range between light and dark tones in an image. A dull, flat image can benefit from increased contrast, but don't overdo it! Applying too much contrast can eliminate the middle tones that add depth and detail to an image.

Color Changes

Overall color changes provide easy-to-apply dramatic effects.

Convert a color photograph to a black and white or grayscale image for an instant aging effect. Some programs offer options for black and white (often called bitmap) conversions. The most basic bitmap converts each pixel to either solid black or white. It's a great way to create "instant grunge!"

Some programs have a "Desaturate" command that converts images to grayscale and keeps the image in RGB mode. This is handy for converting single layers or selections of a color image to gray.

> **low-tech tip**
>
> Another way to quickly create a grayscale or bitmap print from a color image is to select "Grayscale" instead of "Color" under print options. Check "Paper Type/Quality" under the Print menu to see what color and quality options your printer provides. You may also be able to adjust the overall saturation, brightness and color tone of your print.

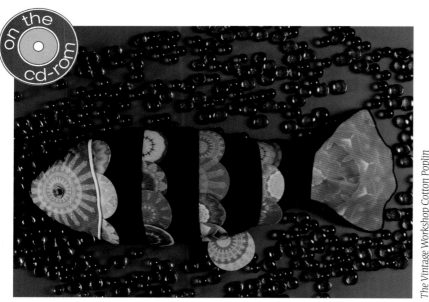

The Vintage Workshop Cotton Poplin

Changing colors allows you to extend the use of your images almost infinitely. This fish pillow uses only four kaleidoscope images, but variations trick the eye into seeing many more. All the images and project instructions are on the CD-ROM.

CD-ROM image coneflower.jpg

Convert a color image to grayscale or black and white for an aged or altered look.

Convert images to sepia tones reminiscent of antique photographs, or tint images with other colors. This is an easy way to avoid clashes when working with multiple images or to match images to a particular color scheme you have in mind.

Sepia tones add a vintage look to photos and illustrations.

ScrapSmart, Victorian Fashions

Two for Tea

To tea dye fabric, you'll need a large pot, tongs or long handled spoon, mild detergent, and black tea or coffee bags.

Soak printed fabric in cold water. Bring two to three gallons of water to a boil in the large pot. You will need enough water to cover your fabric and then some. Tie several tea or coffee bags together, and add them to the pot. Boil for at least 30 minutes. Boil longer for a darker dye. Remove the tea bags from the dye solution, and remove the pot from heat. Add wet fabric to the dye. Allow the fabric to steep in the dye for several hours or overnight, stirring occasionally. When the fabric is a few shades darker than you'd like (remember that fabric looks darker when wet), remove the fabric from the pot and rinse in cold water until the water runs clear. Gently hand wash in mild detergent and rinse again. Lay flat to dry.

Color Cues

Tint images by painting printed cloth with a light wash of fabric paint or watered-down permanent ink. Following manufacturer's directions, lightly apply paint or ink to the images as desired. For a softer look, wet the fabric before applying paint. To create an aged effect, wrinkle the fabric after painting. The paint or ink will settle into wrinkles as it dries. A variation on this technique is to apply paint or ink to wet fabric, then drape the fabric over a textured surface (such as patterned metal or wire) to dry.

Apply color changes to portions of an image by selecting a specific area or color, or by replacing one particular color with another. Some software programs have this feature to reduce redeye in photographs. Use color balance to change the overall mix of color or remove a color cast. Increasing contrast in an image exaggerates differences between light and dark tones; decreasing contrast muddies tonal differences, creating a mysterious, subdued look.

Printed Treasures Sew-On Fabric

Experiment with paint effects on printed images.

Use contrast to define or decrease boundaries between image elements.

Shift color balance to remove an unwanted color cast or enhance certain tones.

Functions, Filters and Effects

Some image-editing programs are so packed with options that the design possibilities seem infinite. A few of the most common effects are shown here.

Overprint images by sending the same fabric sheet through the printer several times. Keep in mind that you probably won't be able to line up images exactly on multiple passes. Registration differences make each print unique. Print the lightest image first, as a light image won't show when printed after a darker one. Place images in different areas of the page, either onscreen or by sending the opposite end of the fabric sheet through the printer on subsequent passes. Give the ink time to dry between printings to avoid over-saturating the print.

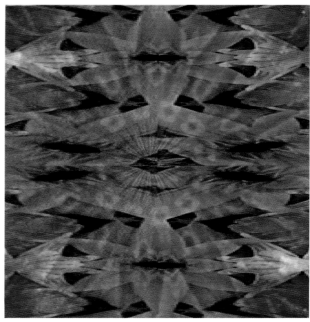

Kaleidoscope Kutz images

Overprinting can result in a batik-looking print.

Electric Quilt Cotton Satin

Use the coin scan image to create this handy soft dish — the project instructions and coins.jpg image are on the CD-ROM. Use an image altering technique for the outer dish and a scan for the inner dish — they coordinate, since they began with the same design.

Gradients are gradual blends from one color to another. Some programs provide fill options for gradient blends, so that colors transition in linear, radial, angled, reflected or diamond shapes. Gradients can be applied to entire images or to selected portions of an image.

Facet, fragment or add half-tone effects with pixelate filters. Pixelating creates clumps of like-colored pixels, which reduces detail in an image.

Photoshop's Diffuse Glow provides a softly filtered, unfocused effect. Check your image-editing program for a similar filter. Softening the focus or blurring detail in selected image areas can direct the viewer's attention, and reducing detail in an image lends a dreamy or mysterious look.

Similar to the cut-and-paste function on a word processing program, cloning portions of an image copies a selection and reproduces it elsewhere. Cloning is great for covering up unwanted elements and 'erasing' photographic mistakes. Repair damaged fabric, providing it's out of copyright, by scanning and replicating intact portions of the cloth.

Layer, stack or combine different elements to add instant image depth.
Create a digital collage or alter images to tell your own story.

Get into grunge by applying various filters to degrade images or text.

 Achieve similar looks by distressing the fabric to physically remove portions of the image. Bleach, sandpaper and selective sun fading can yield interesting results.

Focus blurry images with sharpening filters. By increasing the contrast of neighboring pixels, sharpen filters create the illusion of a more detailed image.

Fade images by adding a white overlay or selecting a transparency option. This effect is especially powerful when combined with a gradation — one image will appear to fade into or out of another.

Think inside the box, or circle or any other shape your program allows! Place images and text into specialty shapes and print as is, or layer with background imagery to create virtual appliqué.

Use shaped masks to create fun photo shapes. See right image also.

ScrapSmart image, Roosters, Hens and Chicks

CK Ltd. dog photo

Resists

Remember the unprinted areas left by thread stuck to the fabric sheet? You can use this effect to your advantage in numerous ways. Ancient textile arts of batik and shibori use varying resist methods to produce patterned fabrics.

This effect is often called masking in image-editing programs. A digital mask blocks out a portion of an image, so only a certain area is printed. You can replicate this with low-tech methods. Use adhesive labels, stickers or tape to block areas of your fabric from absorbing ink. Masking shapes can be cut free-hand or punched with die-cut tools from scrapbooking or craft stores. Stencils make excellent shapes for resist printing. Use varying widths of tape to create stripes and grids. Create artful edges by tearing, pinking or using a wavy cutter on labels or tape. Temporary spray adhesives make instant masks of lace, netting and paper doilies. Masking certain areas of a printed image helps you avoid oversaturating your print and adds placement control.

June Tailor Colorfast Sew-In Inkjet Fabric Sheets; Santa image, Home Arts

Printing over torn painter's tape creates a decorative edge.

Scans in Motion

Achieve unique effects by moving items on the scanner bed while the scan is in progress. Use a layer of acetate against the glass to protect against scratching. You will get different results each time you try this technique!

Slightly moving the item produced a motion-blur effect, while continually moving the item created a unique texture.

Frames

Use an image-editing program to create a picture frame for your favorite photo. Select a design element and repeat it around an opening shape of your choice to create the frame. Print the frame on canvas or another fabric, and trim the opening shape. If the trimmed fabric tends to ravel, apply a seam sealant to the cut edges. Embellish the opening as desired. Center a photo within the opening, and back as desired.

Option: Import the photo into the frames file, and print the photo and frame on one piece of fabric.

Frames don't have to be only for photos — they can frame words and other copy as well. Just open a text box and start typing.

If you want to frame your pet pictures separately without using software, print our no-sew Fabulous Frame projects on the CD-ROM.

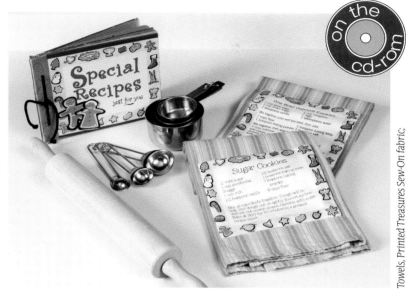

Frame a favorite recipe for a quick gift idea. Project instructions and recipe.jpg image are available on the CD-ROM.

Towels, Printed Treasures Sew-On fabric; recipe book, The Vintage Workshop Cotton Canvas and Cotton Poplin fabrics

Kevin May "Lucy" dog photo; Mary Ann Duff, "Ms. Misty" cat photo

CHAPTER 6
PRINT POSSIBILITIES

Once the printing bug bites, you will think of all kind of things to print on, from lace to twill tape. Some work, some don't — it depends on your printer and technique.

Jacquard Products Cotton

Customize projects for any special occasion — like the loss of a first tooth, a wedding, etc. The recipients are usually in awe that you printed fabric on the computer. For project directions and the images for this tooth fairy pillow, see the enclosed CD-ROM.

Narrow Nuances

Printed ribbons, trims and tapes add a unique touch to many projects. Look for 100% cotton or silk ribbons, laces, twill tapes and trims, or other natural fiber notions. Flat trims with a smooth, printable surface yield the best results. Expand your search beyond the fabric shop to include scrapbooking stores, where trims are sold in prepackaged collections instead of by the yard.

Line 'er up

If the ribbon or trim will be washed, prepare materials just as you prepared the fabric in Chapter 3. Using a dry iron, press narrow printables flat. The width of the ribbon or trim will determine how wide you can make your text or images. Use lettering on narrow flat trims for embellishing scrapbooks and journals, or as gift ties and attachments. Using the ribbon or trim width as a guide, create a file and print a test page on paper or cardstock. Printing in landscape mode will allow you to make longer pieces of printed trim.

Use double-sided tape, or spray trims with temporary adhesive to adhere ribbon or trim directly on top of the printed test page. If necessary, tape down long edges of trim, keeping tape out of the image area. Reprint the file, changing print settings as desired. Let printed trims "cure," and rinse according to manufacturer's directions.

It's best to leave a little wiggle room when working with narrow materials. Chances are that a second printing of the same image will not line up exactly, no matter how carefully you feed the page into the printer. The wider the trim, the more successful you'll be.

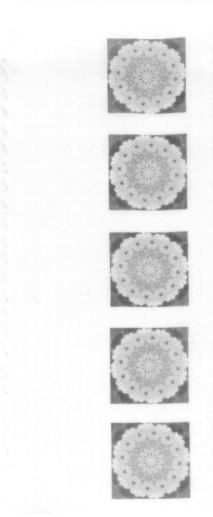

(Twill tape) type; (Eyelet trim) CD-ROM image kkpurple.jpg

Labels

A label is a great finishing touch for any design. Quilt labels record information about the quilt, its maker and when it was made, along with fun sentiments and care instructions. Garment labels may identify the tailor or seamstress, or indicate the current owner of the piece. Create gift tags for personal items, or hang tags if you exhibit your work.

A number of label-making programs are available, or you can make labels using any basic graphics program. Import images, borders or frames into your file, and include any important text information. A fusible web backing or peel-and-stick fabric makes applying your label to the finished piece a snap.

If a label isn't enough space to tell the story of your quilt, consider journaling on the fabric for the quilt back. Write a story, and include other photos or images significant to the quilt story.

CD-ROM image dogfrmbk.jpg; Stephanie Corina Goddard dog photo; Snickerdoodle Daisybear image

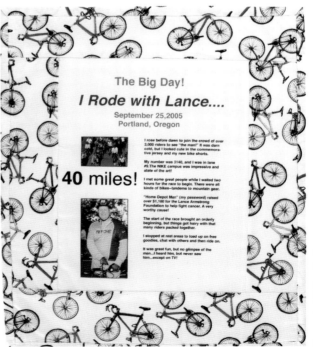

Blumenthal Cotton Poplin

Keep Your Options Open

Don't limit yourself to tried-and-true materials. When the "What if … ?" bug bites, jump right in. Explore local fabric stores for alternative textures and materials to use. If the finished item isn't meant to be washed, you won't have to pre-treat it for printing, and you may prolong its life with a protective sealer or spray.

Fusible Web

Make appliqué patterns by printing on double-sided, paper-backed fusible web. Make sure the fusible has protective paper on both sides, and leave the paper in place while printing. Do NOT put exposed web through the printer, as it will gum up your machine. You may need to touch layers lightly with a warm iron to hold them together.

When the print has dried thoroughly, rough cut appliqué shapes ¼" outside the printed lines. Remove the unprinted paper and press it onto the wrong side of the fabric. Cut out the appliqué on or just inside the printed line, and remove the protective paper. Fuse the appliqué in place according to the manufacturer's directions.

Note: If necessary, mirror-image the appliqué before printing so it faces the right direction.

CD-ROM image ScrapSmart letters.jpg: felt, Electric Quilt Cotton Satin

Fuzzy fabrics like felt reduce the image clarity.

Fuzzy Stuff

What about wool felt, cotton fleece or batting? Some printers will accept the slightly thicker "fuzzy stuff," and others will not. Your printer may be a good candidate if it has adjustments for very thick papers and a direct-feed system to send prints straight through rather than curl them around a roller. Images printed on textured or printed materials will be more blurred than their non-fuzzy counterparts — but that just makes them more intriguing.

Netting, Lace and Sheers

Printing on open weaves like netting or lace is likely to render your printed image unrecognizable — but it can create interesting effects! Printed laces add color and artistic flair to a project. Be sure the fabric is securely adhered to the backing stabilizer, and use "fast" or "draft" print settings and lower ink volume to avoid over-saturating the print.

Lace is available in a variety of fibers as individual elements, trims and yardage. Cotton netting can be found in the bridal/heirloom or millinery section of fabric stores.

Sheers are available in a variety of weights, textures and fibers, such as combed cotton lawn, gauze, voile and harem cloth, or silk chiffon, crepe, gauze and organza, and all can be treated for printing. Or, use Jacquard Products ready-to-print ExtravOrganza.

Use these specialty prints in scrapbooking layouts, altered books, cards and collages, or anywhere you'd like an ethereal effect.

Cotton gauze, Dharma Trading Co.; CD-ROM leaves images

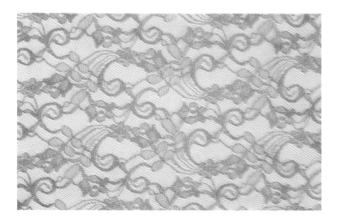

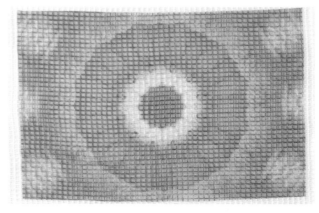

CD-ROM images (silk net) kkpurple.jpg (lace) kkcrocus.jpg

Foundation Piecing

Quilters can create their own foundation or paper-piecing patterns by printing designs on water-soluble stabilizer. Reverse or mirror the design in your editing application. Use a light ink volume setting, and print the design. The stabilizer should feed through the printer easily. After the block is pieced, dissolve the stabilizer according to manufacturer's directions.

Needlework Bases

Preprinted canvas is common for needlework, cross stitch and other hand stitching. Create your own canvases by printing designs on stitchery fabrics, Aida cloth and lightweight needlework canvas. If you're planning to use a portion of the printed image as a visible element, pre-treat the fabric, or post-treat it with protective spray to prolong its light-sensitive life.

Stabilize lighter fabrics with a backing material. When working with even-weave fabric, such as Aida cloth, be sure to cut the piece according to woven lines and feed it squarely into the printer so the design is properly aligned.

If printing on openwork canvas, make sure the mesh is held firmly in place by the stabilizer before printing. Select "draft" or "fast" print modes to avoid over-saturating or smearing the image. Tighter mesh sizes may print better images.

Allow printed canvas to dry completely before handling or stitching.

Without a fixative, any visible ink should wash out of the fabric. Once your stitchery is complete, simply rinse the piece.

Printed Treasures Sew-On Fabric; Flower image, Shepler Studios

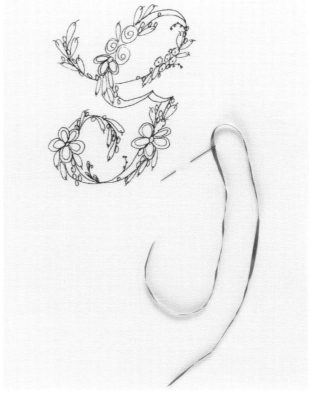

Home Arts Victorian Monograms

Print patterns on untreated fabric, and then rinse away after stitching.

Moving On ...

What if you venture beyond fabric printing? Once you've gotten a taste for it, you'll probably see "printables" all around. Office and art supply stores are filled with specialty papers, magnetic sheets, decals, puzzles, transparencies and even wood veneer just waiting to be incorporated into printable art. Make jewelry from metallic sheets, fashion zipper pulls from heat-shrinkable materials, personalize coasters, mousepads, mugs, etc. Use these as accessories to match your printed fabric creations. Open up to the possibilities, and never stop asking, "What if ... ?".

Inset fabric into a wooden tray for table elegance. The Kaleidoscope Kutz image is on the CD-ROM.

CHAPTER 7
BIG IDEAS

Let's face it — not everything you'd like to print will fit on a letter-sized sheet of fabric, and sometimes those seamlines don't fall in the most convenient places. So what do you do? Super-size it. Check your printer and software for banner, tiling and poster options.

Sandwashed cotton broadcloth, Dharma Trading Co; CD-ROM leaves images

Multiple prints were pieced together to form this jacket lining. Instructions and leaf images for this Deconstructed Denim project are on the CD-ROM.

Banner Printing

Scarves, table runners, quilt panels — these are just a few projects that are perfect for banner printing. Generally, banner printing is the best option anytime a continuous length of fabric makes more sense than several seamed pieces.

Fabric

Several types of ready-to-print fabrics are available by the roll for continuous printing. Silk, cotton and linen comes in various weights and widths. Some fabrics are packaged as kits for specific purposes. Necktie kits contain pre-cut paper-backed bias fabric in 8 ½" x 57" sizes, and scarf kits feature fabric in 8 ½" x 66" cuts.

You can also prepare your own banner-sized lengths of fabric by following the basic steps in

Plan It Out

Take time to plan your project and make the best use of your fabric. Remember the rules of bias and straight of grain. Quality ties are cut on the bias so the tie knots well and hangs nicely. Make sure a purchased kit contains what you need.

Banner printing is perfect for making scarves.

(Blue) Color Textiles silk habotai, Kaleidoscope Kutz image; (Multicolor) Color Textiles silk crepe de chine, Adobe scarf

Chapter 3 and using full-sheet labels, freezer paper or banner paper for backing stabilizers. If using individual adhesive backing sheets, be careful to abut or allow a ⅛" overlap along label edges. Larger overlap areas may print darker and be noticeable on the finished piece.

Cut fabric slightly wider and longer than the finished size, apply backing, and trim fabric to fit with rotary a cutter. Be sure the fabric is securely adhered and wrinkle-free along the entire length. Keep the fabric as flat as possible before printing.

"American Sew with Sue Hausmann" photo

Joe Hesch, Sue Hausmann, Herb Hausmann and Shauna Beatty have fun with banner printing on the Hewlett-Packard segment of "America Sews with Sue Hausmann" television show. Notice Herb's tie and Sue's scarf showing family photos.

Printing

Banner printing requires patience. Large images mean large file sizes that may print slowly. It's best to have a friend help support the fabric as it feeds in and out of the printer.

Test-print your image on the "draft" ink setting by taping standard sheets of paper together along the 8 ½" edges, or print on purchased banner paper. Banner paper, available at office supply stores, is a long length of paper perforated and folded at 11" intervals.

The banner fabric must feed squarely into the printer. Any misalignment will become exaggerated as printing progresses and may cause fabric folds or printer jams. Support the fabric as it feeds into and exits the printer, making sure that the printed end doesn't inhibit the inbound material.

Don't despair over printing problems. You can seam together smaller images, and you don't have to super-size your printing every time. Start with shorter lengths to learn the nuances, and gradually work your way up to a larger size.

Be Warned!

You must have a software program and print driver that support banner printing. Not all programs and printers support banner, tiling and poster printing options. Even though a printer may list these abilities, it may not work with your particular program or system software. Consult your software and printer manuals for instructions on banner settings and size limitations, or contact technical support for your printer. Include a description of the sizes you want to print and your system and software program information. Some programs automatically set the print size based on file parameters, while others require you to create a custom print size based on the dimensions you'd like to print. Some programs designate banners in 11" standard letter-sized lengths.

Printing large pieces of fabric can use a lot of ink. If possible, insert a new ink cartridge before printing to be sure you won't run out.

Tiling and Poster Printing

Some software programs provide tiling and poster options for printing oversized files. Both options divide an oversized file into sections based on the selected paper size and parameters. Some programs offer options for adding crop or trim marks, overlap and registration symbols. Others allow you to choose the number of tiles or pages to print. The image is printed on a number of pages or fabric sheets, which you can piece together to create a larger sized print. For example, a 2 x 2 tiled image prints the image two tiles (or pages) wide by two pages long. A 2 x 3 tiled image prints two tiles wide by three tiles long.

Because the computer automatically divides the image, page breaks may not be placed in the optimum spots for stitching. A seam down the center of someone's nose is not an artistic touch! Check the "page preview" screen or test print to see where page breaks fall. Alter the portrait/landscape orientation, or choose a different tiling option to shift page breaks.

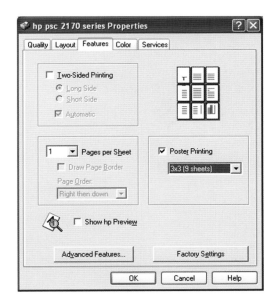

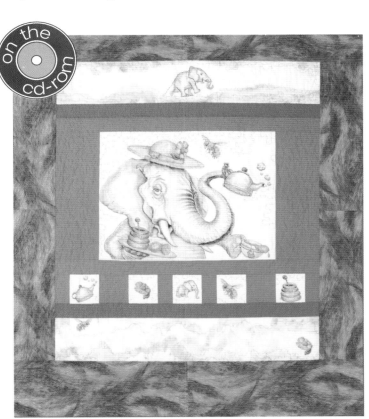

Oversized images can be printed in sections and seamed together. Project instructions and images for this fun kid's quilt appear on the CD-ROM.

CD-ROM Shepler Studios elephant images

Search for poster+software on the web to discover independent poster-making programs. Some software can create images up to 100 feet square. However, enlarging images to this size will likely result in pixelled pages.

Some programs allow you to tile your file manually, so you can choose how an image is divided.

Another option for printing tiles is to create an oversized image in your image-editing program, then select page-sized portions to copy and paste to individual documents.

Whichever printing method you choose, don't forget about seam allowances! Leave at least a ¼" margin on all sides to stitch individual prints together.

 Plan ahead to enlarge images with poster or tiling options. Start with a high-resolution file so that the image won't become blurry or lose detail when enlarged. Scan images at a high resolution, such as 600ppi (or dpi) or greater, (or at larger than 100%) to create useable images for poster-sized prints.

CD-ROM elephant images

If possible, put page breaks in less noticeable places.

Lay out the pieces of your large design in the proper sequence before joining them.

The Vintage Workshop Linen

Piecing Posters

There are several ways to stitch tiles or poster prints together. The most common methods are sashing for a windowpane effect and continuous for a single image look. For each method, lay printed pieces out in the proper position to plan your stitching. The size of the image in each section is related to the original image proportion and the fabric size used for printing.

Sashed Piecing

Adding sashing or strips of fabric between printed pieces increases the overall size of the finished project and reduces any worries about perfectly matching images at seams. Since sashing provides a buffer between individual prints, any slight misalignments are less noticeable.

Continuous Image

Create the look of a continuous image by carefully joining printed pieces together. Lay the pieces face up to determine the seamline. Edges may have distorted during the printing process. You may need to align the images with a deeper seam than planned.

Finger-press a seamline on one printed piece, making sure that some of the image is included in the seam. From the right side, align the printed pieces. Pin the pieces together, inserting pins vertically at the top and bottom of the seam. Turn finger-pressed fabric to the wrong side and re-pin horizontally along the seam, taking care to keep the images aligned. Stitch on the finger-pressed seamline, removing pins as you sew. Check alignment before trimming the seam allowances.

If you have trouble keeping the images aligned, you can temporarily hold the folded seamline edge in place with a washable fabric glue stick or water-soluble basting tape.

Kaleidoscope Kutz image

Invisibly seam poster printed sections together.

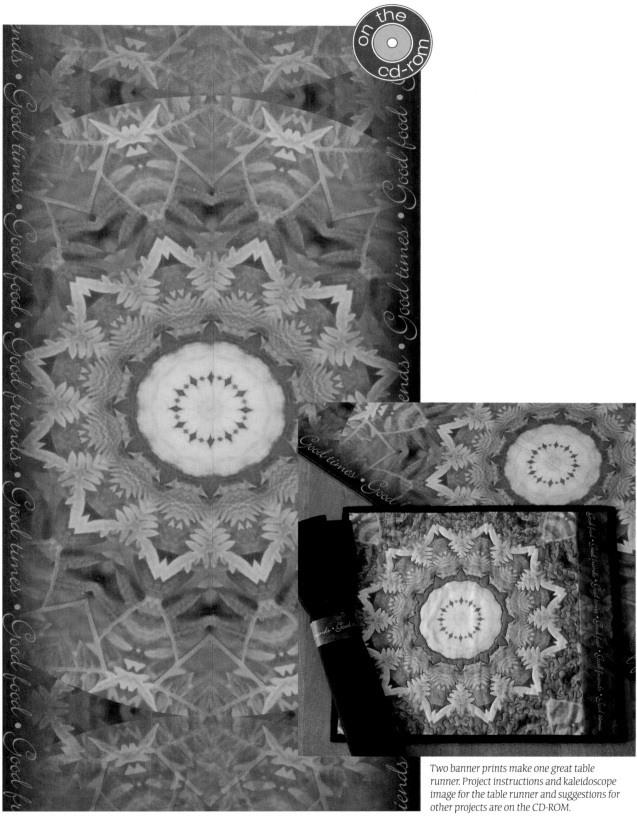

Blumenthal Cotton Twill, Bubble Jet-set treated Egyptian cotton and Fredrix Sew Paintable Canvas; CD-ROM image kkferns.jpg

Two banner prints make one great table runner. Project instructions and kaleidoscope image for the table runner and suggestions for other projects are on the CD-ROM.

CHAPTER 8
NOW THAT IT'S PRINTED

Playing with new techniques and media can unleash your creative side. But what do you do with all those wonderful, inviting prints?

Water techniques: Summer Vacation: Janet Klaer photo, Fredrix Sew Paintable Canvas; Resist techniques: June Tailor Colorfast Sew-In Inkjet Fabric, Home Arts images; Colorizing techniques: The Vintage Workshop Linen, Miss Mary's Quaint & Curious Clip Art; Text effects: Blumenthal Craft Cotton Poplin

Small projects like postcards are a great place to try out a myriad of new techniques. There are lots of opportunities for creative exploration without a large investment in fabric or ink. Look for images and the project directions on the CD-ROM.

We've created more than 20 inkjet fabric printing projects on the enclosed CD-ROM for you to try the various techniques in the book, but we have only scratched the surface of what's possible. We hope that we've encouraged you to go beyond the book and step into the "What if … ?" world for yourself.

Playing with Water

Some interesting effects can be created by altering printed designs with water. Results will vary, depending on the fabrics used and how quickly your ink dries.

Working over a sink or on a protective surface, experiment with the prints. You can:

- Use an eyedropper to place individual water droplets on the printed surface. The ink will dissolve, and droplets will become slightly discolored. Remove excess water with a cotton swab.

- Lightly wet various objects, and press into the image surface to push ink around or lift it away.

- Wet a paintbrush or toothbrush and flick bristles with your thumbnail to splatter the printed surface lightly.

- Scrub the image surface with a damp cotton swab to lift ink away. Use inked cotton swabs to 'paint' an image or add color in other areas.

- Holding the print over a sink, use a squirt bottle to create drips or a wash effect.

- Hold the print under running water or quickly submerge the print in water for an overall wash. Use caution, as it is easy to wash the ink completely away.

Let the images dry completely.

Hang the images outside or in a well-ventilated area, and spray with two or three light coats of matte finish to seal the prints.

Button Up

Need an accessory for a special outfit? Print an image for a covered button. Cut your image in a circle big enough to cover the button mold. A short mist of adhesive spray on the button cover will help keep the image centered while you finger-press the fabric in place and secure the button back. Work side to side and top to bottom to attach fabric, slightly stretching the material for a smooth, tight fit. You can use large button forms to create ornaments.

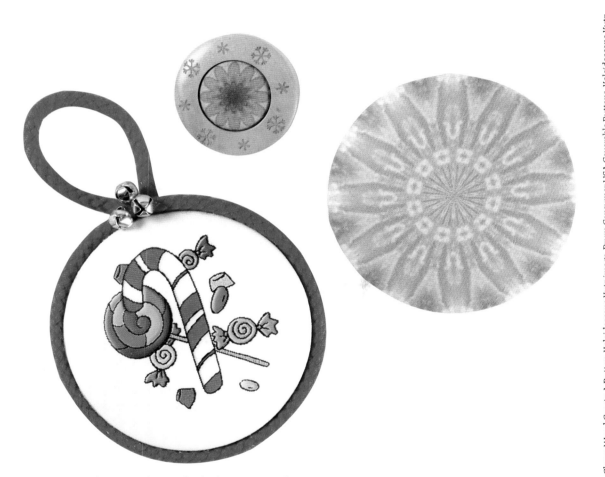

Clover Wood Create-A-Button, Kaleidoscope Kutz image: Prym Consumer USA Coverable Buttons, Kaleidoscope Kutz image: ScrapSmart Christmas Fun image

Experiment with images and various kinds of cover-your-own buttons.

In Your Face

What's more fun than purchased dolls? Personal ones! Print and place a child's face on a simple stuffed doll or mini-quilt for hours of playtime fun. A child will love a "mini-me" even more if he or she is dressed in matching clothing, so don't forget puppet potential as well.

Sandy Ahlgren Sapienza doll

Sandy Ahlgren Sapienza quilt

Go 3-D

Add dimensional interest to printed images with accent fabric, yarn, beads, ribbon, trim, buttons, buckles, iron-on crystals and other accents. Hand or machine embroidery provides additional texture. Just for fun, dress up a body shot with a tutu or hula skirt.

Electric Quilt Cotton Satin

ScrapSmart's Antique Letters (letters.jpg) is easily highlighted with lace, ribbons and charms. See instructions for this project and the image on the CD-ROM.

Janet Klaer photo

Add gathered net and a ribbon flower to give dimension to this ballerina print.

Iron-on Embellishments

Press-on accents come in a variety of shapes, sizes and finishes. Use a hot-fix applicator tool to secure them in place exactly where you want them.

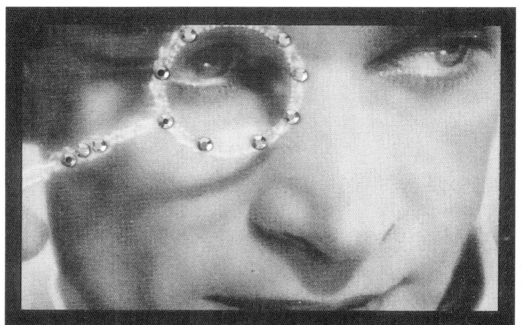

Artchix Studio photo, Kandi Corp. crystals

Annette Bailey photo, Kandi Corp. crystals

Iron-on crystals accent printed photos.

Machine Embroidery

Stitched accents can be used to highlight printed backgrounds. Print first, and then hoop and stitch using pre-programmed stitches or free-motion work.

Husqvarna Viking offers 3D Sketch software with printable images and the capability of adding free-motion look stitchery to enhance the print.

Combine machine embroidery with a printed fabric background. Use computerized embroidery motifs or free-motion work to accent the printed photo elements.

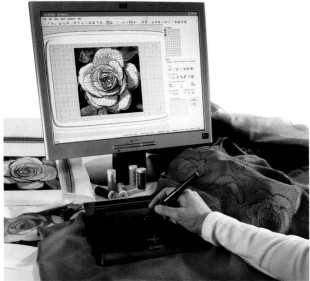

Husqvarna Viking photo

Husqvarna Viking 3D Sketch samples

Color It In

Create a coloring book with printed line art. Set your inner artist free with fabric paints, paint sticks, markers, crayons and chalk. Make sure your inkjet prints are dry and the coloring medium can be used on fabric before applying color. Protect your coloring surface with newspaper, cardboard or a plastic sheet. You could even let the kids play, too!

Stay inside the lines — but only if you want to!

Printed Treasures Sew-On Fabric; Schiffer Publishing, Art Noveau Era Graphics

Tuck It In

Printed fabric images are perfect inserts for pre-made vinyl products like checkbook covers, luggage tags, bookmarks and more. Lights, pens, purses and other media make personalized gifts and showcase your printed imagery at the same time.

Trim the printed fabric to the template size included with the product, and tuck the trimmed piece inside. If necessary, fuse the image to interfacing before cutting for added stability or opacity, or leave the carrier backing on.

Insert printed fabric into ready-made items.

Cottage Mills Pix Pen, CD-ROM image kkcrocus.jpg; Traditions Studio mug, Stephanie Corina Goddard dog photo; Z Becky Brown bag, CD-ROM image The Vintage Workshop clematis.jpg

Overlay

Add mystery to an image or tone down a glaring print with an overlay. Lightweight sheer fabric, lace or netting can be layered over a printed piece, and if left unstitched along one edge, can instantly create a treasure pocket. Scrapbookers use this technique to include journaling, notes, tickets, trinkets and other treasures to complement images in their work. For added effect, print the overlaying fabric, too!

Add texture with printed and layered lace, netting and organza.

Jacquard Products Silk and ExtravOrganza, June Tailor Sew-In Inkjet Fabric Sheets

Rev Up a Ready-made

There's no rule that your printed images have to be placed on made-from-scratch sewing projects. Dress up ready-made sweatshirts, jackets, tees, totes, purses and gift bags with your print work. Depending on the base fabric, you may sew, fuse or glue prints to your projects. Follow the manufacturer's directions to fuse items to wood, metal and other surfaces.

Highlight image edges with decorative scissors or cutting blades on no-sew applications; simply apply paper-backed fusible web to the wrong side of the fabric, decoratively cut, peel the paper and fuse it in place, making sure the edges are anchored securely.

Note: To fuse pieces on inaccessible areas, use a seam roll, sleeve board or wooden piece placed inside the item as an ironing surface.

A ready-made denim jacket is the perfect canvas for images like these from The Vintage Workshop Clothing Collage and Chic Bag Boutique Click-n-Craft CDs.

Little Tiny Works of Art

Even the smallest portions of printed images can be collaged with other elements to create tiny works of art. Fuse miscellaneous items together, or sandwich bits and pieces between microscope slides, antique optical lenses or discarded picture frames.

Take it Home

Printed pieces make perfect additions to your home décor. Create instant wall art with printed canvas or decoupaged prints, print a pillow or encircle a room with a wallpaper border. Showcase your printed images in pre-made accessories designed for needlework insertions.

Printing your own fabric makes it easy to create coordinating items for your home. Project instructions and the Allover elephant image are included on the CD-ROM.

June Tailor Sew-In Inkjet Fabric Sheets

tip

Removable Wall Images

Soak printed fabric in liquid starch, then apply to the wall. Smooth away wrinkles with a brayer or large sponge. To remove, carefully pull fabric away from the wall, and wipe away any residue with warm water.

Scraplight lamp

Make a lamp for your sewing room using the sewingsq.jpg image on the CD-ROM and inverting the color.

Kaleidoscope Kutz image

Frame a print with silk for an upscale pillow.

Fractionated Fun

Back an image with fusible web, and then rotary-cut the print into slices. Put it back together and fuse to another fabric background, leaving a little room in between. Embellish as desired to create a one-of-a-kind work of art.

For a different creative option, apply fusible bias tape over an image to create crossing lines. Depending on placement, the bias tape adds a windowpane or stained glass look.

CD-ROM image flower.jpg

Back the image with fusible web, spread onto a background, and then fuse in place.

Blumenthal Lansing Recycled Ancestors image; Clotilde's Sewing Savvy photo

Narrow braid separates the photos printed on a single fabric sheet.

Recolor and resize the four kaleidoscope images from the CD-ROM to create a mini-quilt with fusible bias "sashing." The "quilt" is printed on a single sheet of fabric.

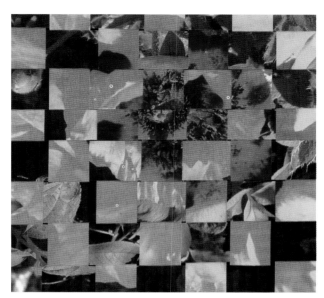

Weave strips into fractionated works of art.

Weave It In

Cut multiple prints into random strips to create a woven work of art. If desired, apply fusible web before cutting the strips, and then fuse the finished fabric together; or, print on fusible fabric for an even faster intertwining. Your woven projects will make wonderful mini-quilts, place mats or wallhangings — or combine them to create larger pieces of unique fabrics. Think about weaving together family photos and then trying to figure out which parts belong to whom!

Original photos used in the weaving above — same flower, different views.

Piece a panel

Stitch together scraps or misprints to form blocks for a small quilt or garment.

Use a single motif for all kinds of applications — from a pocket to a garment yoke. Nothing should ever go to waste; rather, scraps should be viewed as creative opportunities.

Printed Treasures Sew-On Fabric

Printed images are perfect for tote bag pockets. Project instructions and sewingsq.jpg image are on the CD-ROM.

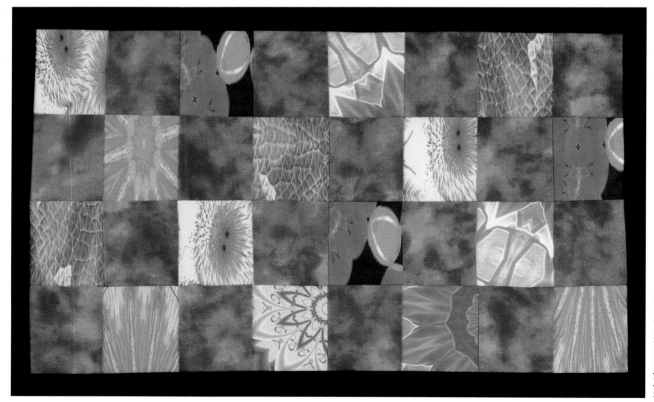

Kaleidoscope Kutz images

Pick a Patch

Patches aren't always hiding a flaw — they can be purposeful, and with fusible printable fabrics, it's a cinch to decorate simple bags for any occasion.

Printed images also make perfect patches, and they can be decorative or functional as well. Pretty botanicals embellished with beads are perfect to hide flaws and dress up any pair of jeans.

The ultimate hostess gift is a favorite beverage in a lovely bag, but don't stop there — add a snack bag full of treats as well. The wine.jpg image and project instructions are on the CD-ROM.

This place is a zoo, but stop by for tea!

Add coordinating prints to build on a single printed patch.

Draw It On

Fake an appliquéd look on fusibles, or simulate the look of stitching (either decorative or straight) with a permanent fine-tip pen. Fabric markers come in a variety of colors and widths, and they are great for adding details such as lines, stitches, stippling and random marks.

Go Ornamental

Incorporate bits and pieces of less-than-perfect prints into holiday ornaments. Simply substitute printed pieces for whatever fabric your pattern requires. Make a quick textured garland — layer printed scraps with batting, and chain stitch them together with decorative thread. Embellish a gift bag, or craft an all-occasion card with extra elements.

Search Press, "Decorative Initials"

Let the kids color their own printed patches, and add faux blanket stitching.

June Tailor Quick Fuse

Print and stitch your own all-occasion card.

Quilt on the kaleidoscope design to create a wonderful bag. Project instructions and the kkpurple.jpg image are on the CD-ROM.

The Vintage Workshop Cotton Poplin

Iron-on vinyl adds sheen to the knitting tote pocket. See the CD-ROM for project instructions and the yarn.jpg image.

Printed Treasures Sew-On Fabric

Stuff It

Add dimension to your printed image by adding batting or stuffing under it. Simply put another layer under the print (either fabric or batting), and stitch around portions of the design. If you used batting, trim away the batting outside the stitched shape. If you used fabric, carefully cut a slit in only the backing layer, and lightly poke stuffing into the stitched shape. Whipstitch the slit opening closed.

Or, back your print with batting, and stitch on the design lines of the print.

Slick Tricks

Iron-on vinyl can add brilliance to less-than-stellar printed fabrics. Available in both matte and shiny finishes, it simply irons on over the fabric, offering both protection (think child's bib) and shine. Just follow the manufacturer's instructions to apply and care for this fun addition.

CHAPTER 9
TRANSFER TACTICS

As much as we'd like to think we could print on anything, sometimes it just isn't possible. But that doesn't mean you can't embellish fabric — and more! — with transfers.

Iron It On

Some fibers won't accept ink, and other items just won't fit through the printer. One way to get around these obstacles is to transfer the printed image to the fabric or item where you want it.

In the past, transfers have changed the hand or feel of the fabric, making it shiny, stiff and unpleasant to stitch with, much less wear. Some products still produce those undesirable results, but others have improved so that transfers don't significantly affect the fabric's feel.

Several types of iron-on transfers are available, and some work better for particular applications than others. There are transfers for light or dark, or knit or woven fabric. Other transfers have special effects, such as holographic or glow-in-the-dark imagery. Some transfers are brand-specific and won't work well with other types of inks. Be sure to purchase the right transfers for your printer type. Laser and inkjet varieties aren't interchangeable. Check office supply, quilt, craft and fabric stores for available options.

Transfer materials may be opaque or transparent, either blocking the background fabric or allowing it to show through.

Read manufacturer's directions carefully. Some transfer sheets require images to be printed in reverse; others do not. A few manufacturers recommend pre-washing the fabric or garment to remove sizing that could interfere with adhesion; others suggest pre-warming the base before transferring the image. For the most polished appearance, trim the transfer material close to the image to avoid having a large border surrounding the image.

Hard Pressed

Proper pressing techniques are critical to successful transfers.

- Press on a hard surface, not a padded ironing board. Most transfers require you to use medium- to high-heat settings on a dry iron. Check the manufacturer's suggestions for iron settings.

- You may need to use a press cloth to avoid scorching.

- Use firm, even pressure, and pick up the iron and move it instead of sliding it to another area. Sliding the iron may distort the image or wrinkle the fabric.

- Press each section for the recommended amount of time. Do not hurry this process!

- When pressing is complete, you may either peel the paper backing away while the transfer is still warm ("hot peel") or wait until the transfer has cooled ("cold peel"). Check transfer instructions for product recommendations.

Peel the paper backing in a smooth, even motion. If the transfer hasn't adhered properly, you may need to replace the paper and re-press.

Use transfers to apply motifs over a print fabric.

Lucy Gray Veggie Lover's handbag, reprinted from DRG's "Sewing Basket Fun"; Dover Publications image

Transfer Care

Never iron directly on the transfer material. The heat of the iron will melt the transfer and make a mess on your board. If you must press the project or garment, use a non-stick protective press cloth and a light touch.

To wash a project, turn it inside out prior to washing, and use a detergent without bleach or optical brighteners to help prevent fading. Wash in cool water and hang to dry. Some transfers may melt in the dryer.

(Red) The Vintage Workshop Iron-on Transfer 2, Celebrate America image; (White) The Vintage Workshop Iron-on Transfer 1, ScrapSmart Gymnastics Style image

Caution: Creativity Ahead!

Printing your own fabric is one of those activities that ought to come with a warning label.

Creativity can be wonderfully addictive! Once you start wondering "What if … ?" a world of possibilities will open up, and you'll see printing opportunities everywhere. A walk around the block may yield a treasure trove of textural items to photograph or scan. Rummage sales and thrift shops are sure bets for interesting — and inexpensive — fabric finds. And ideas for applying printed images are absolutely endless.

Are you into embellishing? Quilting? Scrapbooking? Combine printed fabric with your other passions and increase your creative options! Personalize garments, gifts, and home décor. Create one-of-a-kind items with your unique prints. Paint, dye or sun-print fabric. When dry, print over the top of your art, and then continue the creativity by coloring with markers and paint or removing image portions with water or bleach. Not satisfied with the results? Start the process over again. There's no right or wrong way. You decide what works or what doesn't and when to start and stop.

Not every image or print will become an immediate masterpiece. Save those less-than-perfect prints for future projects. You may be able to salvage a portion of the print or reprint over the initial image. Misprints make great canvases for trying new techniques, because you won't be afraid of "messing up" the image.

Most of all, *have fun.* Don't fret over flaws or inexact experiments. Just enjoy the journey, and never stop asking yourself "What if … ?".

little bits of inspiration • little bits of inspiration

little bits of inspiration • little bits of inspiration

About the Authors

Linda Turner Griepentrog

Linda was the editor of Sew News magazine for 19 years and currently owns G Wiz Creative Services (so named because no one can pronounce her last name).

Linda writes, edits, plays and sews for a number of companies in the sewing and craft industries. In addition, she leads fabric shopping tours to various destinations in the U.S. and abroad. Working from her basement office, Linda lives outside Portland, Oregon with her husband Keith and two dogs, Riley and Buckley.

Missy Shepler

Missy made the leap to her own home-based business after years of working as an illustrator, graphic artist, designer and technical support person. She now commutes across the lawn to Shepler Studios with her husband Scott — and far more fur-friends than she cares to admit to having. Most of her days are spent staring at the computer screen, pushing pixels around, and drawing, designing, writing and working on client Web sites. Whenever possible, Missy escapes upstairs to the sewing studio to stitch, embellish and just have fun with fabric.

Projects on the CD-ROM

Instructions and images for these projects are on the CD-ROM.

Adobe Acrobat can be used to view the projects, patterns and artwork on the CD-ROM. Acrobat can be downloaded from the Adobe Web site free of charge.

All projects, patterns and artwork on the CD-ROM can be printed at full scale on an 8 ½" by 11" standard printer.

A BAG FOR ALL REASONS

These bags are perfect for wine, treats, soles or scents — just pull the strings!

WINE TOTE & SNACKER BAG

MINI SACHET

SHOE BAG

CANVAS CADDY

Great for carrying garden tools, this durable canvas bag totes groceries and more.

COIN HOLDER

It's the perfect place to toss change, jewels, buttons or baubles.

CASE CLOSED
Use these handy zip-top holders for anything and everything.

COSMETIC BAG

QUILTED BAG

SEWING BAG

DECONSTRUCTED DENIM
Replace worn patches with personal prints.

ELEPHANTS AT LARGE!
Cute prints and quick piecing make these projects special.

QUILT

PILLOWCASE

 LAMPSHADE

 Indicates a no-sew project!

EVERYDAY INSPIRATIONS
Perk up your paperwork!

FUSED FILE FOLDERS

JOURNAL COVERS

PORTFOLIO

FABULOUS FRAMES
Any pet lover will love these adorable photo frames.

GO FISH!
This pillow is fun and funky for home décor — or as a big pincushion in the sewing room.

KITCHEN CUTUPS
These dish towels do double duty!

SEWN

FUSIBLE

MAKING MEMORIES
Create a special remembrance for any occasion.

SEWING/KNITTING TOTE
Use these sturdy and spacious carryalls for your favorite hobbies.

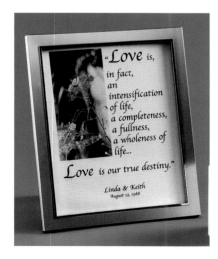

MAT-TER OF FACT

These simple place mats decorate and teach.

LEARNING PLACE MAT

SILVERWARE PLACE MAT

TABLE FOR TWO

Show off your art at the table with banner printing.

PILLOW PIZZAZZ

The Tooth Fairy will love it!

THE EYES HAVE IT

Store your specs safely and stylishly.

TINY TREASURES

These postcards are the perfect size for trying new techniques.

VICTORIAN ELEGANCE

ScrapSmart Antique Letters accent this mini shoulder bag.

BONUS!
DOUBLE-FOLD BINDING

BONUS!
TECH TIPS

About the Artists and the Art on the CD-ROM

Alison Winn

The owner of Studio 513 in Manchester, Iowa, Alison loves note cards and creates her own line of personalized cards featuring a variety of hobby motifs, including sewing and knitting. Contact Alison at studio513@iowatelecom.net.

blueshoe

sewingsq

fork
knife
silvware
spoon

cosmetic

Mellisa Karlin Mahoney

A publishing company photographer by day, Mellisa loves to look through the camera lens and capture the beauty of what she sees. In addition to her day job, she sells her work as a freelancer through MKM Studios. Contact Mellisa at mkmsutterbug@aol.com.

flower

hibiscus

Micky Turner

Micky enjoys photographing with a unique vision to find the extraordinary within the ordinary views of things all around us. She incorporates unusual techniques such as 3-dimensional stereography, extreme macro and teleidoscopy. Through her business Kaleidoscope Kutz, she sells image CDs to artists, sewers and crafters. Contact Micky at KaleidoKutz@msn.com.

kksilk

kkcrocus

kkpurple

kkferns

Contributing Companies

We're pleased to include designs from ScrapSmart (letters.jpg) and The Vintage Workshop (clematis.jpg) on the CD-ROM. Both companies continue to support our efforts to spread the word about the fun of fabric printing. Look for many more images and information about all their products at www.scrapsmart.com and www.thevintageworkshop.com.

The Vintage Workshop

clematis

ScrapSmart

letters

Scott and Missy Shepler

Working together as Shepler Studios, Scott and Missy Shepler provide design, illustration, and editorial services to a variety of clients. Both Scott and Missy are big fans of wondering "What if … ?". Contact Scott and Missy at info@sheplerstudios.com.

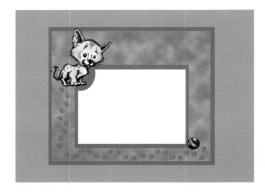

catfrmft
catfrmbk

dogfrmft
dogfrmbk

eyeglass

wine

recipe

zooquilt

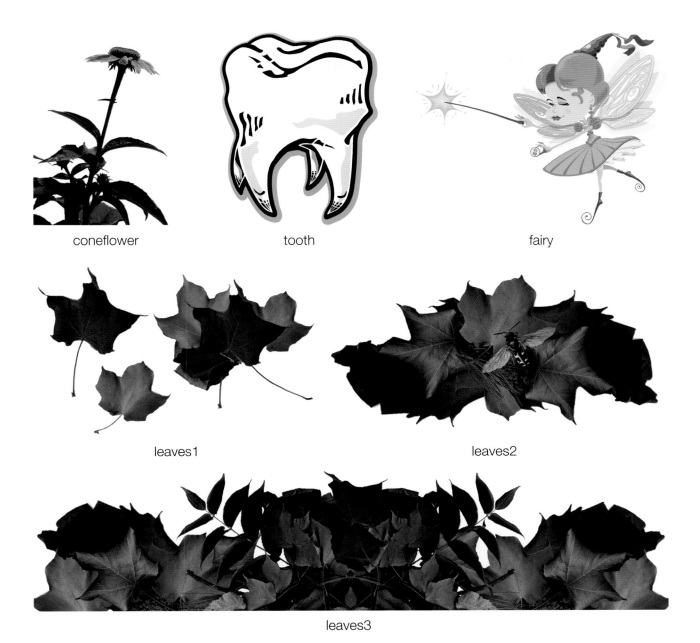

coneflower

tooth

fairy

leaves1

leaves2

leaves3

Bonus items!

You'll find these extra tidbits in the Bonus folder on the CD-ROM.

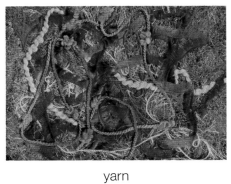

yarn

coins

Resources

Many resources are available for inkjet fabric printing supplies and images. This list is by no means all-inclusive, as technology changes daily. For additional resources, search the Internet and check your local fabric, craft, quilt, art and office supply stores for new products. The companies marked with an asterisk contributed products or photos for this book — thank you!

Software

Adobe Systems, Inc.*
www.adobe.com

ArcSoft
www.arcsoft.com

Corel Corporation
www.corel.com

Electric Quilt Company*
www.electricquilt.com

Kaleidoscope Collections, LLC.
www.KalCollections.com

Microsoft Corporation
www.microsoft.com

onOne Software
www.ononesoftware.com

Photoshop Elements Techniques
www.photoshopelementsuser.com

Picasa
picasa.google.com/index.html

Poster Software
www.postersw.com

Quiltsmart*
www.quiltsmart.com

Image & Typeface Sources

Adobe Systems, Inc.
www.adobe.com

Art Chix Studio (preprinted images)
www.artchixstudio.com

Blumenthal Lansing*
www.blumenthallansing.com

Canon Print Planet
www.canonprintplanet.com

Clipart.com
www.clipart.com

Craft Computer Paper
www.craftycomputerpaper.co.uk

Design Originals*
www.d-originals.com

Dover Publications*
www.doverpublications.com

GraphXEdge
www.graphxedge.com

Hewlett-Packard (Quilt Label program, Scrapbook Assistant program, downloadable imagery)*
www.hp.com

Home Arts*
www.ezhomearts.com

Husqvarna Viking (3D Sketch)*
www.husqvarnaviking.com

Kaleidoscope Kutz*
kaleidokutz@msn.com

Kathy Schmitz*
www.kathyschmitz.com

Miss Mary's Quaint & Curious Clip Art*
www.missmary.com

National Geographic
www.nationalgeographic.com

Quick Art
www.quickart.com

Schiffer Publishing*
www.schifferbooks.com

ScrapSmart*
www.scrapsmart.com

Search Press*
www.searchpressusa.com

Snickerdoodle Dreams*
www.snickerdoodledreams.com

The Vintage Workshop*
www.thevintageworkshop.com

Two Peas in a Bucket
www.twopeasinabucket.com

Veer: Visual Elements for Creatives
www.Veer.com

VV's Victorian Prints*
www.vvprints.com

Printable Fabrics, Transfers, Supplies

Blumenthal Lansing*
www.blumenthallansing.com

C. Jenkins Necktie & Chemical Company (Bubble Jet Set)
www.cjenkinscompany.com

Color Textiles
www.colortextiles.com

Dharma Trading Co.
www.dharma.com

Electric Quilt Company*
www.electricquilt.com

Fredrix*
www.fredrixprintcanvas.com

Jacquard Products*
www.jacquardproducts.com

June Tailor*
www.junetailor.com

Mallery Press
www.mallerypress.com

Printed Treasures*
www.printedtreasures.com

PrintOnIt.com
www.printonit.com

PROChemical & Dye
www.prochemical.com

Sew Paintable*
www.sewpaintable.com

Soft Fabric Photos
www.softfabricphotos.com

The Vintage Workshop*
www.thevintageworkshop.com

Specialty Supplies

Clover Needlecraft (wood buttons to cover)*
www.clover-usa.com

Cottage Mills (Pix Pen)*
www.cottagemills.com

Crafter's Pick (The Ultimate! Glue)*
www.crafterspick.com

Creek Bank Creations (100% cotton twill tape)*
www.creekbankcreations.com

Dick Blick Art Materials
www.dickblick.com/

Fairfield Processing Corp. (Poly-fil)*
www.poly-fil.com

Kandi Corp. (iron-ons and hot tool applicator)*
www.kandicorp.com

Krylon (fixatives)
www.krylon.com

Pellon (interfacing/stabilizers)
www.shoppellon.com

Plaid Enterprises (Artistrywear)*
www.plaidonline.com

Prym Consumer USA (buttons to cover)*
www.dritz.com

Ranger Industries (Inkssentials Memory Frames)
www.rangerink.com

RNK Distributing (Floriani stabilizers)*
www.rnkdistributing.com

Scraplight (lamps)*
www.scraplight.com

Sudberry House (wood products)*
www.sudberry.com

Sulky (temporary spray adhesive)*
www.sulky.com

Therm O Web (iron-on vinyls and fusible adhesives)
www.thermoweb.com

Traditions Studio (clear mugs)*
www.traditionsstudio.com

Tristan Embroidery Supplies (Aurifil threads)
www.tristan.bc.ca

Warm Company (batting and paper-back fusible webs)*
www.warmcompany.com

Weeks Dye Works (overdyed floss and threads)
www.weeksdyeworks.com

Wisconsin Lighting (self-adhesive lampshades)
www.wilighting.com

Z Becky Brown (clear purses)*
www.zbeckybrown.com

Other Web Sites for Fabric Printers

Ami Simms
www.amisimms.com

Caryl Bryer Fallert
www.bryerpatch.com

Clotilde's Sewing Savvy/"Sewing Basket Fun"
Published by Needlecraft Shop/DRG Publishing
www.clotildessewingsavvy.com

Gloria Hansen
www.gloriahansen.com

Quilting Images
www.quiltingimages.com

Soft Expressions
www.softexpressions.com

Yahoo Discussion Groups
http://groups.yahoo.com/group/BJSFabricPrintingFX/ (Bubble Jet Set)
http://groups.yahoo.com/group/inkjet_transfers/ (Inkjet Transfers)
http://groups.yahoo.com/group/inkjetfabricprinting/ (Inkjet Fabric Printing)

Get Creative and Have Fun With Your Fabric!

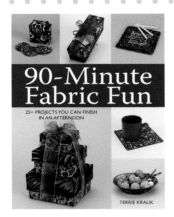